THE LIFE 101 PROJECT

BOOT CAMP FOR THE SOUL

BY
GAYLON KENT

The Life 101 Project:
Boot Camp For The Soul

Copyright © 2024 by Gaylon Kent

All rights reserved. No part of this book may be reproduced or transmitted in any form or by any means without written permission of the author.

thelife101project.com
gaylonkent.net

For Terri, Autumn, and Ming-Dao
Proteges and Master
Both with lessons

FOREWORD

There are two types of people in this world: those who get what they want out of life and those who do not. Those whose hearts are content and those whose hearts are heavy with regret.

You might think the former is the exclusive province of the rich and famous, of those you watch or read about. Compared to them, you might even think a contented life is beyond your grasp. Nothing is further from the truth.

Those who get on in this life can be anyone - from a champion athlete to the person who fixes your car. The one trait they share is they are in complete control of their existence. They are following their hearts and trusting their instincts. They are maximizing the talents they were issued at birth. They make their time serve them, instead of serving time while on this planet. This book will show you such a life is there for everyone, including, especially, you.

To a novitiate, any spiritual discipline can seem perplexing and mystifying. The purpose of this book is to demystify what it takes to live the life you were put here to live. There are no deities to pray to, no sacred texts to read, no church or temple to give money or time to. There is only you, your inner self, and the 24 hours each of us has every day, the only commodity all of us are issued in equal measure.

This book is divided into three sections: Wisdom, Courage and Patience. Each trait is valuable on its own, of course, but they work best together and those who get on in this life possess and utilize all three: they have the wisdom to know what they are about, the courage to live the life they are meant to live and the patience to do this every day.

It is never too early or late to start. Those who are young will have the benefit of many years on their Paths, while more experienced readers will have the benefit of being able to use the wisdom and context offered by past years and experiences.

It is a journey that is both easy and hard. Easy, because you do the things you enjoy and have a knack for. On the other hand, it is supremely difficult because we must do these things every day, without fail, from the day we make a spiritual commitment until the day we die.

This book will show you how to make the commitment and take the journey without burning incense or wearing robes or chanting for hours on end, though you can do these things if you want to.

Those on The Project ask for nothing more than living the life they were put on this planet to live. They also demand nothing less. By doing this you will come face to face with yourself, scary for some, but soon to be the great delight of your life. You don't have to be brilliant; you don't have to live down the ages – though some do – and you don't have to be great.

You only have to be you.

So let's go. The life you are meant to live awaits.

TABLE OF CONTENTS

Wisdom 1
Courage 42
Patience 82

WISDOM

As one thinketh in his heart, so is he.
King David

Wisdom is the foundation of life on your Path because we cannot make our time serve us without knowing what we are about. And it doesn't take as much work as you might think; some time listening to your heart generally provides the required insights into yourself. Wisdom comes before Courage and Patience because without Wisdom, Courage and Patience will do you little good.

King David's quote is true enough. We humans have an astonishing capacity for getting out of this life what we expect to get out of it. Those that expect little generally get little. Similarly, those that expect good things generally get them, too. Every good thing in this life starts with knowing what you are about.

Dawn
There are a variety of dawns in the world. There's the personal dawn of our birth. There's the dawn always waiting for us tomorrow, and then there is the dawn that attends a spiritual awakening. This is the dawn you are experiencing today.

You had a choice today: you could easily have done something else, what you have been doing for years, perhaps decades. By choosing your Path, you are choosing to know and to maximize your inner self. You are choosing to get in tune with the life you are meant to live.

Every dawn brings a choice: are we going to conquer doubt and weakness or are we going to surrender to those two imposters? Are we going to follow the dictates of our inner self or are we going to ignore them? Are we going to utilize our time and talents or are we going to squander them? Are we going to mark time, or is time going to serve us?

It is not possible for a life spent on one's Path to be futile. A person fully absorbed in The Project, by definition, lives the life they are meant to live - life's great prize. At every new dawn, we sign up for our Path. It's our way of announcing our time on this planet is serving us.

Dusk

The end of the day is the respite from the day's labors and cares. Like every other hour of the day, it is time our Path allows us to put to use.

Did we accomplish today what needed to be accomplished? Were we focused or did we allow outside distractions to take precedence? What did we comply with: the commands of our inner self or the dictates and whims of others? Did we put nature and circumstance to work for us or did we fit into the slots assigned by others?

Night is a good time to answer these questions. If we did well, it lays the foundation for tomorrow's triumphs. If we could have done better, it provides the inspiration to conquer tomorrow's 24 hours instead of squandering them. When we've faced ourselves honestly we are poised for a good rest. We awake prepared for the sun's rising and the new day.

Oneness

While those on The Project respect all spiritual paths, they remain certain the only way to achieve oneness with all things is to achieve oneness with themselves. They long ago decided they could not do this by producing knee-jerk reactions to outside influences or trying to fit into slots assigned by others. All living from the outside in got them was frustration because their inner self was being ignored, their time and talents squandered. They were out of touch with themselves, with others, and with the rest of the world.

You have decided you've had enough with being out of touch with yourself. The road to oneness begins with the wisdom to know what you are about. This involves self-examination, a journey to the center of your soul to determine the talents you were born with and how best to put them to use, a journey not everyone is willing to take.

Summits

Too often we think in terms of one attainment being an accomplishment for a lifetime. Of course, there are summits in every life, but we can't let one attainment be the end-all of our time on this planet. Our Paths have many summits for us, but we do not stay on them forever. We arrive, enjoy the view for a bit, look back on the vision and work that got us there, and then we leave, to find another summit to climb.

Some live for one moment and that is regrettable because once that perceived golden moment is achieved, nothing else will measure up. Their day is done even though there may be many years before their life is done. Those on their Paths make their entire life their moment. Attainments are nice, but there must not be one that tops all others. One summit merely leads to another.

Cycles

Life is a series of cycles, each of which has a beginning and an end. A cycle running its course usually gives notice of its impending termination, and it's good to pay attention to this for a couple of reasons. One, we do not want to end a cycle prematurely and miss withdrawing every possible benefit from it; two, we do not want to linger in circumstances that have run their course.

We must be in tune with ourselves, tuned into every nuance offered by our Path. When we are, we'll know when a cycle has run its course and, in time, realize that one door closing invariably means another is opening. Those on their Paths handle an end with the same poise they handled its beginning and the attainments and struggles that followed.

We must be without prejudice and prepared for whatever comes our way. We remain on our Paths because we can see the big picture and because we have the focus required to see the current cycle through to its conclusion.

Nature
There is little we can do when nature is determined. We are powerless. When nature is of a mind to cause havoc, it will, without regard for who or what is in its way.

While we are powerless over nature, wisdom is the first step toward having complete power over ourselves. We can choose to be weak, meekly accepting what life and others choose to spoon-feed us, or we can choose to be strong, a force unto ourselves, somebody who is making their time serve them, a person who has overcome themselves.

When we have the wisdom to know what we are about, we are in step with nature. It may overcome us one day, but it does not control us, it merely guides us.

Bias
It's not easy giving up prejudices, which can run the gamut from biases toward people to certain cuts of meat. It is part of our collective human experience to find our biases comforting.

When we do give up our prejudices - sometimes shared by others - it shows we have overcome portions of ourselves. It means we are different from others, and some will not take that well because when we decline to fit into the slots offered by others, we are taking a road less traveled. This makes others who are fitting into their assigned slots uncomfortable

Those on The Project realize that prejudices limit their development and constrict the benefits withdrawn from every experience. We remain on our Paths for a variety of reasons; obtaining and retaining an open mind is one of them.

Divinity

Taoists think of their life as divinity itself. Not because it's holy or should be heralded by others but because it is theirs. They can't live anyone else's life - nor do they want to - and no one can live theirs. Their life is divine because it belongs to them, because they are the only person they see every day, because they are the only one who knows what they are about. Those on their Paths know what they get out of this life is - to an extent that surprises some - dependent on the work, diligence, and courage they put into making good things happen for themselves.

Knowledge

There is no substitute for knowledge and the only knowledge that matters is knowing yourself. People who go through life feeling a half-step off or frequently scold themselves for going against their better judgment find themselves this way because they are out of touch with their inner selves. They spend their time reacting to external elements and squashing the voice inside commanding them to maximize the talents they were born with.

Instead, circumstances close around them, like a cell door. They are not expressing the very core of their being and it is left lying dormant, not doing them or anybody else any good.

Those working The Project know themselves and, as such, journey to their very core every day. Not some days and not others, not some weeks and not others, not some years and not others: every day, from the time they commit until the day they die. They've listened to their hearts and know exactly what they are about.

Longevity
Our Paths guarantee nothing except the life we were meant to live. This does not mean we are going to merely take what comes and accept a second-rate life. Nothing is further from the truth. Every day, those on The Project look inside themselves, determine what they are meant to do, and then go and do it. But they realize life is long and remain prepared, eager, and willing to go the distance.

There is no time frame for anything, and we must have the wisdom to accept and embrace the years, knowing our Paths will take us exactly where we are meant to go.

Heart
Those on The Project learn to listen to their hearts. This is the sum total of every experience, lesson provided, word read, and meditation conducted. The only real lesson we have to learn is to block out external factors that prevent us from reaching the very core of our being, and we must accept nothing less than living the life that comes from following our hearts.

It doesn't matter what that life is, either. All of us were issued assorted and varied talents at birth. It could be anything, from writing a book to making a quilt to building a chair because no one else is you and no one else is me. Time on your Path will show you how to maximize your talents so when the time comes to examine your life, you will realize you did well and did not squander your time on this planet.

When we succeed in our hearts, we have reached our summits.

Past

The past has been revered since time immemorial. In fact, honoring and even worshiping the dead is the foundation of many traditions, religions, and of many spiritual disciplines.

And the past must be respected. It's the views, actions, conflicts, and triumphs that got us to where we are today. We must respect their summits, just like we will request future generations to acknowledge and respect our summits. Indeed, a society or family that has lost touch with its past has lost touch with itself.

But we must not be mired in the past. The past is there to be learned from, to be scorned and admired as required, but it is not to be imitated. We must blaze our own trails. Though past masters might show us various aspects, it is up to us to identify and follow our own Path.

Learning

The years offer wisdom and context, and those who get on in this life never stop earning their share of wisdom and context. Our minds – to paraphrase the 14th Dali Lama – are like parachutes, working best when open. Those on The Project know that knowledge can be found anywhere, and they are careful to keep their minds open because the meaningful can turn up at any time, and they don't want to miss it.

As we engage our Paths, the lessons nature and circumstance have shown us over the years take hold. Wisdom shows us our strengths and our weaknesses, what we can do well, and what we are better off leaving to others. Since we know our strengths, we are free to utilize them. Since we know our weaknesses, we are free to steer clear of them.

Solitude

For those on the Project, the greatest fear is leaving a desired road untraveled. Of course, this is a solitary pursuit – as it should be because no one hears our inner voice but us; we are the only ones who can walk our Path.

Those on The Project, however, are not hermits and they are careful to pay attention to the people that cross their Paths. They need others just like others need them because others help them know themselves. It's one way we ensure we are comfortable in our own skin.

Wisdom

Wisdom is an interesting animal: people want it and admire it, but few go and get it. This is too bad because wisdom is literally there for the taking, waiting for anyone willing to seize it.

Some chase wisdom through formal education, and this is admirable because, of course, we must know things; little of substance is accomplished without significant knowledge. We must know what we need to know and what we want to know and then go and find these things out, but even those in the finest universities will squander their time if all they do is take notes and pass tests.

Wisdom is earned, not dispensed. It comes not from mastering a course of study but from mastering ourselves.

Connection

Everyone needs to believe in something larger than themselves, and they need to connect with it. We call it your Path, and there are other names for it, too, like the natural order or the always so. Every religious affiliation, every spiritual discipline, and every self-help book is an attempt to connect with this larger order. Most depend on external sources to deliver a contented life.

The Project teaches that these external sources are superfluous. Everything we need to connect with the larger order is inside us, and the only barrier to our inner self looks us in the mirror every morning. Are we going to spend our day on our Path, or are we going to spend our day reacting to outside influences? Are we going to fritter away our time and our talents, or are we going to maximize them? These are the only questions that matter, and those on their Path are committed to connecting with themselves every day.

Harmony

Those in harmony with themselves may give the impression they are living without being dragged down. Now, as you gain time on your Path, you will find you are no more immune to the travails and inconveniences of everyday life than anyone else is; however, as the influence of external factors are minimized, you will be more and more at peace with answering to your heart.

We have all seen the smallest events send those without any spiritual guidance whatsoever reeling. These people are not in harmony with themselves, so all is chaos because their entire time is spent reacting to events and people.

You are putting the work into knowing the life you are meant to lead. When you spend your time living that life, you will find yourself in harmony with yourself.

Independence.

Everyone expects things from us. Employers, family, friends – it's rare when someone accepts us for who we are with no expectations because this makes them comfortable. We fit snugly into the slot they have assigned us. When we don't fit into assigned slots, we are deviant and treated accordingly, and it is difficult to be treated like this. It's the way the world is built.

We should embrace independence because there is more to life than compliance with the dictates of others. We have one opportunity at this existence, and we must be determined to make a go of it. The independence some shy away from is exactly what those on The Project embrace.

Triumph
There comes a time when we've withdrawn every possible benefit from a circumstance, situation, or experience. It could be something that's lasted a half-hour to a week or even several years. Perhaps we've become about as good as we are going to get at something or have accomplished all we care to. It doesn't matter.

What matters is that we recognize these times and realize that sticking with something would mean merely hanging around. Those on their Path are keen to recognize these times, and while the ending might be poignant, they are met with relish because it means they are liberated to move on to the next cycle in their lives.

Oneness
Oneness comes when we no longer make a conscious decision to be on our Path because we are doing it automatically. We don't need to ask whether something is or is not what we should be doing with our lives. We don't need to consider whether or not actions are in accordance with nature. We don't wonder whether or not our time is serving us.

This is oneness, a life lived from the very core of our being. We have become one with ourselves.

Question
Those who get on in this life chased the dreams of yesteryear just like they are chasing the dreams of today. They have the wisdom to know when their time comes to die, they will

ask themselves if their time on this planet served them or was it wasted? It is the only question that matters, though in the rush of everyday life, we might not realize that.

Those on their Path have made the commitment to answer that question with a yes.

Vitality

It's a long life for most of us, and it's easy to get into ruts, where one day looks like days past and, soon enough, the years start to look alike, too. Before anyone knows anything, decades are all looking eerily similar as well.

People remain on The Project because they avoid ruts. We are regularly shown fresh prospects, and since we are conditioned to put nature and circumstance to work for us, we see where fresh prospects lead. When we do this, we remain a vital, dynamic, compelling presence in our own lives.

Discovery

Regularly there are new roads for us to travel. Sometimes whether or not to follow these roads is obvious. For example, an opportunity we've long worked for must be seized; concerns over success and failure must be put aside because they are mere imposters; take one away, and the other vanishes, too. Similarly, something that gives us immediate pause or doubt should probably be avoided. After even modest time on our Paths, we will find that our instincts are generally trusty.

Equilibrium

Geese flying together establish perfection without even trying. There is not a lead goose measuring the distance between everyone and they don't have a committee consulting a map. They simply set the course nature gave them and follow it, the distance between them, as well as their ultimate destination, automatically taken care of as nature takes them exactly where they are meant to go.

Geese have lessons for us. Those who get on in this world let their Path take them where they are meant to go. Like the geese, they do not fight nature and dare not try to control it because just as nature takes care of her geese so, too, do our Paths take care of us, allowing us to flee the desert and chase the summit.

Introspection

Introspection is the relentless, daily process of looking inside ourselves and deciding what we should be doing with our time on this planet. Those that do this find their Paths while those who do not practice introspection ignore their inner selves. They may attain some external satisfactions but ultimately miss out on the life they were meant to live.

When we follow our hearts and trust our instincts, when we live from the inside out, we are taking the only journey that matters. Few others will care what we do, so we have to care. The Way will always show us where we need to go.

Possibilities

Some approach spiritual self-cultivation as a panacea for misfortune and when The Way – or any spiritual path, for that matter – does not produce immediate superficial wonders, they wander away after only a short time.

People who do this miss out on the meaning of The Project: it does not lead to the end of the rainbow, merely to the life you are meant to live. There are no deities or gospels or prophets, only the work we put into constructing a useful and meaningful life.

The Distance

We must go the distance every day, from the time we make the commitment to self-cultivation until our time is done. All 365 days of a year are going to pass, and the only real decision we have to make is how we are going to spend those days. The Project teaches that 365 good days will lead to a good year, good years will lead to good decades, and good decades will yield a good life.

Making the decision to start is easy. Then comes the work of self-cultivation, and going the distance seems like an awfully long way to go. For some, the wisdom, courage, and patience required to walk their Path seems like more than they are capable of giving.

Give it. Every day. Because once some time on your Path is gained, what were once difficulties and sacrifices are now habits that are embraced.

Modesty
There is modesty, and there is false modesty. The former is good; the latter is not.

We are entitled to enjoy our attainments. We earned them, worked hard for them, and we are not aesthetics: it's OK to enjoy what you earned. The only ones who cherish false modesty are those who have nothing to be modest about.

Modesty also demands that we acknowledge there are things we cannot do because the first rule of The Way is to know ourselves. But to deny talents, skills, and attainments, to be modest about things you should not be modest about, does not do anyone any good. We must use modesty to push us forward, not hold us back.

Loneliness
Some think loneliness comes from not being in contact with others. Nothing is further from the truth: it comes from not being in contact with yourself. Loneliness comes from the

inside, from not being comfortable with oneself, from being out of touch with what you are about. Despite the company of others, there might be a gnawing feeling that there is more to life.

Those on The Project are not lonely despite, perhaps, being alone. They know what they are about and, therefore, are comfortable with themselves. When this happens, loneliness turns into solitude, something to be appreciated and, at times, treasured.

Meaning

What we give meaning to defines our lives. Those who give meaning to outside influences, mindless revels, and superficial friendships invariably wonder, "What if?" Doing nothing of substance has earned them nothing of substance.

We must give meaning to the things generated by the very core of our being. Anything else is dismissed. When we do this, a meaningful life finds us.

Lotus

The lotus has long held symbolism in a variety of cultures. Its meanings, traditions, and symbolisms differ, though they often center around rebirth and spiritual attainment. This is because of its rather unique life cycle. It lives in water, is rooted in mud, blooms during the day, and retreats into the water at night, only to repeat the process the next day. It can live for many centuries.

We should open our hearts like a lotus, ready to go where it commands us. At night, we retreat to bed, ready to repeat the cycle the following day. We do not live for centuries like the lotus, but when we open our hearts every morning, we live the life we are meant to live, just like the lotus does.

Utopia

Not even your Path guarantees happily ever after. Life is not a novel or a made-for-TV movie. Even those squarely on their Path miss out on utopia because utopia is perfection, and nothing we do is perfect. There will always be a mark that is missed, either because we missed it or a person or event moved the proverbial target.

The battle never ends. Every day there are seventy times seven distractions to knock us off our Path. Or external circumstances change and what has long offered stability and comfort no longer does. The day-in, day-out courage and patience required to accomplish self-awareness, not yield when the easy presents itself, to believe in yourself when there might be doubts, are life's valiant efforts.

Sages

Sages are good at issuing sayings and aphorisms left and right. They have reduced their lives to even fewer things than your average person on their Path and can pontificate on the folly of humanity because, to a great extent, they have removed themselves from it.

Us non-sages, still in the trenches, are not so lucky. There are demands of family, work, and friends. It's helpful here to remember the utter lack of control we have over others, their thoughts, words, and actions. Because we have little control over them, we should also have little interest. When we remember to let go of what we have no control over, we are liberated from the cares and concerns others have, and our minds are calm. We have become sages to ourselves.

Ordinary

The ordinary is disdained by some, but the ordinary remains the foundation of the great and the good. No one goes straight to the summit; there are no shortcuts from the Gobi Desert to the top of Mount Everest.

Wisdom

The ordinary must be experienced before it can be transcended because ordinary effort produces extraordinary results. A step leads to a journey and, eventually, a journey leads to the summit.

Knowing the ordinary is how we know the great.

Attainment

Some are never happy with what they have. An accomplishment is either compared to what someone else did or to something grander they aspire to. It is never enough. It is never something to be thankful for, merely something to be analyzed and compared.

When those on The Project reach an attainment, they are suitably grateful for and content with it. They do not become consumed with it though and, at the appropriate time, they resume their journey, grateful for the work, focus, and accomplishment, but ready for the following summit. Attainments are merely an aspect of their journey.

Intuition

We all need guidance. We only have to look at the self-help collection at a bookstore to see this. Most people contemplating a spiritual quest do not start one, and fewer complete it because some spiritual disciplines are neither simple nor intuitive.

Novitiates following The Way soon realize their Path is completely intuitive. They are not asked to do things that are not second nature, they are merely asked to focus on their inner selves, to utilize and eventually maximize their time and their talents. As they grow on their Paths, they find concentration and confidence literally there for the taking.

Definition

Those on The Program disdain labels and aim to put themselves beyond definition. They realize they cannot do this until they know themselves, until they've looked inside to know and feel what they are about. This is wisdom. As you gain time on your Path, you will come to realize that you have defined yourself and you are leaving others to fit into the slots others have assigned them. You are a unique peg that will only fit into the slots you assign yourself.

Guidance

Some look to recognized scholars, holy people, or sages for guidance, but really, the only guidance we need comes from inside us. True, we all need someone to show us The Way, but like the ship that dismisses its pilot once it leaves the harbor, so too must we eventually set out on our Path on our own. When we've had the courage to do this, all things come to us.

Those with many years on their Paths continue to need guidance, and the wise know this can come from anywhere, from sages to novitiates to those off their Paths. They combine this with their own wisdom and intuition to eventually transcend all things so that they have become themselves.

Acquisition

The always so is neither issued nor dispensed. Awareness of your inner self cannot be gained by the waving of a wand, casting spells, or reciting creeds. Even The Project cannot take you to the very core of your being; you have to do that yourself. All The Project can do is make you aware it exists.

You must go and claim the life you are meant to live. The Project introduces some principles, but you are the one who either claims them or rejects them. There is no middle ground: you are either on our Path, or you are not. Either you have the required understanding to know what you are about, or you do not. Your path must be reclaimed and renewed every day.

Peace

While each day on one's Path is time well spent, from time to time those following The Way will find themselves doing something that is a cut above their daily journey, something that speaks to them from the very depth of their soul. It could be a single moment or last many days. When this happens, you will realize every other day on your Path was a prelude to this, and you transcend meditation and void: we are at one with ourselves and enjoy complete peace.

Decline

It's not easy to acknowledge our decline. We forget things at the store, need something repeated because we didn't hear it correctly, the power on our reading glasses increases, and a condition requires daily attention. These things add up, and before we know it, we've lived many more days than we have left. While we can establish good habits, more decline is inevitable.

Those on their Paths know this is part of The Way. It can no more be fought than our success and attainments could be fought: they were a natural part of our Paths, just like our last day will be. Both should be treated with equanimity.

Form

Starting out in any worthwhile endeavor is not easy. Soldiers need basic training. Carpenters need to know wood and the implements to shape them. A new sports official needs to learn rules and positioning. Even if we are starting something we have a knack for and an interest in, there is much learning involved.

The same is true for those choosing to find their Path. Not even masters and sages were born on their Paths. They were novitiates once, too, needing the same introduction to The Way and encouragement to keep on with it that every other novitiate needs.

Time on your Path yields dividends, though. Your first steps might be hesitant because you are taking a road less traveled and this is not easy to do. If it was, more people would do it. Eventually, though, the effort required to walk your Path is forgotten, having become a natural part of your day. You are doing what needs to be done without second thoughts.

Absolutes

There aren't many absolutes in this life. Individuals come and go. Circumstances change, and ideas and convictions evolve with the centuries, sometimes with the days. Of course, seasons come and go, and years pass.

Even our inner selves change. You will not be the same person you were in your 20s, nor should you be. Those who have changed very little over the decades are marking time instead of progressing and we might accomplish something only to find we've then lost interest in it.

The only absolute is our Path, which ensures we move forward every day. When we do that, our Path pays dividends, taking us one step closer to where we are meant to go.

Seeing

Appreciating a painting is the difference between looking and seeing. Some will look and not be inspired, while others will find meaning for them.

We must look at ourselves and see, too, because we are the artists of our lives. Every day we are issued a blank canvas and every night we must take stock of that canvas. What do we see? Did we do well, or did we waste the 24 hours we were given? Did we put useful strokes on our canvas or did we put a mish-mash of scattered strokes on it?

If we see good things, we must accept and enjoy these good days. If we weren't pleased with our canvas there's use in that, too, because it can serve as a foundation for tomorrow's determination and diligence.

Deception

Both experiences and people can be deceiving at times. Some that appear inconsequential sometimes turn out to be profound. Sometimes the opposite is true: a time long anticipated, and perhaps even worked toward, turns out to be anticlimactic.

After some time on your Path, you will learn to approach all things with equanimity, with experience showing you true rewards appear when expectations are set aside.

Choice

Each day we choose what to do with our souls. Our inner selves beckon and every day we must choose whether to answer this summons or ignore it. Those that get on in this life heed and embrace their summons. Those that wander aimlessly from day to day, year to year, cradle to crypt, ignore it and look back asking what if.

The effects of this decision are felt immediately. Those on The Project, even those just starting out, are setting off confidently on the life they are meant to live. Those who dismiss their inner selves are relegated to days, years and decades squandered.

Determination

Wisdom is not given; it is earned. And it is not reserved for old men with long white beards living in caves or clergy clad in robes, or those with many degrees. It can be earned by anyone because every aspect of this life offers a lesson. Some ignore these lessons while others embrace them, using this knowledge both in the present to learn more about themselves and their fellow beings and filing it away to provide future benefits. Those who do this, regardless of status or station – if they have any at all – find wisdom accumulating as the years pass. They apply it to their lives, an accent to and by-product of life on their Path.

Time

Followers of The Way know that time is one element that cannot be reused or recycled. True, we have a fresh 24 hours tomorrow, but that is merely another canvas placed on our easel; today's canvas is taken away forever. If you see someone on their Path unusually committed to something, this is why: minutes, days, years and decades cannot be recalled for later use. Once time has passed, it is gone forever. Our obligation is to complete our journey and to do that we must use today's minutes and hours to produce worthwhile years and decades.

Rituals

Though you are embarking on a spiritual quest, rituals are not required. Some will have them, and you might well acquire some, but they are at your option. Neither are their chants to learn or texts to read, except for this one. They are ancillary to life on your Path.

The lack of rituals can be frustrating to some, but consider this: anyone can kneel in supposed reverence, receive a sacrament, or chant a creed. Spiritual rituals have their place, but adherents of any spiritual discipline must take care that it does not become a comforting balm that they think absolves them from putting any more effort into their spiritual quest.

Our best ritual is day-to-day living on our Path, wasting neither time nor talents. Our greatest ritual is time well spent.

Existence

The best example that everyone has a Path to follow is someone standing in front of them who is on their Path. Does this person seem to know what he is about? Does this person speak from the heart, or does he prattle about the superfluous? Does he give the impression of peace?

People on their Path do not have any magical skills. They are not wizards, merely someone who is in-step with the life they are meant to live, a circumstance that produces no small measures of confidence and peace. Seeing it for yourself and wanting that for yourself, and believing it is achievable, shows you it exists and is attainable.

Problems

No one is immune to problems. Our Paths, after all, do not offer a perfect life, merely the life we are meant to live, and things both good and bad attend everyone. (Though those on The Project tend to have fewer problems than others simply because they mind their own business.)

The difference is in how problems are handled. Some will deal with a problem with whatever reaction will dismiss the problem the soonest. This does not solve anything; it merely postpones it for later. Those on their Paths ask themselves – automatically after a while – if they are merely putting a Band-Aid over a wound or if they are seeing the entire picture and taking – or avoiding – actions that will actually close the wound.

Clarity
Our minds must be focused, our lives reduced to a few things that matter. Some are misguided as to what those things might be. They spend their time chasing avarice or influence or power or coveting what others have. Their minds are scattered, lacking a point of attack for their life, and they ignore the gnawing inside them that directs them to the very core of their being. After sufficient time doing this, they probably don't even hear their inner voice all that much, and their time has passed, even though they may still have many years to go.

Sanctuary
Everyone needs a sanctuary. This is true not only for sages, prophets, and poets – whose exploits and antics are well known – but for us mortals as well. Any and every place where we connect with our inner self is significant. For some, it's a grand cathedral, a rock by a stream, or even a parked car. Where is unimportant. Why and how are what matter, gifts from our inner selves. Where is merely an external factor.

Whether our sanctuary is elaborate or simple is of no particular consequence; it merely has to mean something to you. Our lives must mean something to us, and for that to happen, there must be places that mean something to us.

Liberation
So much of our identity can be wrapped up in external factors, such as others' opinions, position in an organization,

and status. It starts at birth when we want and need the approval of parents, and those with religious training soon learn they must earn the approval of a supreme being.

The Project, however, demands we look inside. This isn't any easier, either, because we are forced to look at our goals, talents, and fears – at what we really are instead of what others merely want us to be – and work our way through this jungle to produce a constructive life.

This is liberating because we are now free to look ourselves squarely in the eye, content knowing that what we get out of this life mostly depends on the work we are willing to put into it. When we do this, we dismiss the external and the superfluous and embrace the eternal and substantive.

Humility

Some will be envious of your life. Now, the specific circumstances may not cause envy, but the peace that invariably radiates from someone on their Path just might. It is here that humility is one of our most useful tools because it neither seeks nor draws attention.

Those on their Path will find success and sometimes a healthy measure of it, and humility helps remind us this, too, shall pass and that we will not always be at the summit. Similarly, when times are difficult and circumstances, perhaps, reduced, humility helps us realize that this, too, shall pass and life is not entirely spent in a valley.

Power

Sages have been referred to since time immemorial and held to be wiser than some. This is because they have merely become completely familiar with every aspect of themselves. Like sages, we, too, can become completely familiar with ourselves, our journey on our Path falling from us as leaves fall from a tree. Our power has been released, and our lives are spent completely in our element. We are listening to our hearts and following its direction. We do not go against our grain and thus hold ultimate power over ourselves.

Achievement
We've talked about this before: achievement is relative, and success and failure exist only in relation to one another. Take one away, and the other disappears, too. Relieved from the burden of relative and transitory accomplishments, we are liberated to freely and joyfully go where our time and talents take us. Even a short time on our Paths shows the life we are meant to live and success and power have no power over us. When that happens, how can the result be anything other than wonderful?

Intangible
The Way is everywhere and nowhere. It is all around us because nature is all around us and The Way is nature, but good luck reaching out and touching it. It is intangible and an adept talking to a novitiate cannot reach into a pocket and pull out an example.

The Way, our Path, can only be experienced when we open our hearts and minds to our inner selves. It only exists when we open the door and let it in. When we beckon, it comes. When we dismiss it, it vanishes.

Zenith And Nadir
All cycles have a beginning and an end and those who get on in this life become adept at recognizing them. This can be difficult when life is showing us either a zenith or a nadir, a high or a low. No one wants to let go of a moment equally marvelous and rare and the view from the summit can be difficult to surrender. Similarly, nadirs pass, too, though some

find it easy to wallow in them. When you are on your Path, you will recognize both as part of everyday life, and choose not to revel or wallow in them.

Knowledge

Knowledge has always been gained for advantage, to put someone in a better position to accomplish something. This is all right. We humans are meant to grow, to do, and to achieve. We're not meant to maintain the status quo.

As we say here from time to time, Mount Everest cannot be summited by wandering aimlessly around the Gobi Desert. The more time we have on our Paths, the more we know about ourselves, and this means more time ascending the summit than wandering around the desert. Our profit from knowledge is time well spent, the life we are meant to lead.

Truth

It can be difficult to find our truth. It's hard to break away from the pack, to go another way and take a road less traveled. Your truth, however, only begins with your first steps on your Path and you will find good first steps lead to the first good days and these lead to good weeks. Your truth will emerge and before you know anything you have good months and good years under your belt. Doubt about what you should and should not do with your life is eliminated because you are whole; you have discovered your truth, life's great prize.

Expression

Though everything we want in life is on our Path, we must take care to express ourselves quietly. We must not herald the fact we are on our Path. It will be plain to those who care to notice. We must not herald the good fortune of the contended lives our Paths have put in front of us. This will cause scorn and envy. Similarly, we must keep the bad fortune to ourselves, too, because we are not the only ones bearing burdens.

Those on their Path try to avoid causing extreme reactions in others. Because they avoid extreme reactions in themselves, they generally succeed at this.

Distractions

The distractions that knock us off our Paths are relentless. Every day, we must fight the compliance mandated by society to follow some mindless lead. We must fight with our natural, age-old instinct for supernatural comfort for what we cannot explain. Even outside realms like religion and science do not offer completely satisfactory answers to our most basic questions.

The ancient voices we hear are heard by all. It's the way the world is built. It is important that we not try to overcome them. Our battle is overcoming ourselves. When we do this, our most basic question – what are we here for? – is answered. When we've overcome ourselves, we've found our Paths, distractions are relegated to the rearview mirror, and we are going where we are meant to go.

Balance

Now, it is important to note The Way does not give special privileges or favors. It does not offer a secret passage to the end of the rainbow. Your Path will show you good times and bad and show you a course through both, always returning to balance from extreme.

Time here will show you the center of your soul, and you will find rewards equal to the work you've put in. In time, if you're not there now, all you will ask is to get up every morning and make your time serve you. If you hear voices others do not, it is only because you are listening for them.

When you hear your heart, you are liberated to block out the commotion of others and paint your own canvas.

Ego
The ego is an interesting animal. It can keep us from ourselves, but it can also immerse us in the very core of our being.

It's our ego that puts satiation and accomplishment ahead of following our Path. We get selfish and let the superfluous occupy our minds and inner selves. In due course, we are looking back at time squandered.

That same ego leads us to The Way. We get selfish and demand more than the compliance and conformity that attend daily life. We are willing to show the wisdom to know the life we are meant to live, the courage to go and live that life, and the patience to do it every day. Also in due course, we are looking back on time well spent. The same ego that can waste our time also allows us to maximize it.

Obstacle
The wholly human trait of blaming others is one of the biggest obstacles there is.

It's a lesson of The Way, though, that our lives are our responsibility. If we spend our time scheming and treating others poorly or living solely for material gain, we should not be surprised when things do not go as planned or, if they do go as planned, they are not as satisfying as we thought they would be.

Did a plan we made go wrong? Well, sure, it might be easier to blame others involved, but was the plan we made fixed aright to begin with? Did our plan come from something inside, or was it merely a ploy to gain advantage? If someone is hurt, did we do something to cause it? If the plan was right, was our effort true? Before we go blaming others we must look at ourselves. Our aim must always come from the heart.

Today

It's never too late to find The Way. Every day on your Path – even if the first ones come later in life – is a step forward and every step forward pays a dividend. The Way ensures that those following it have bodies and minds that, while hardly immune to age, remain finely tuned for as long as nature permits. We all have things we must accomplish in this life – both great and small – and it is never too late to start ascending our summits.

Years

No one, not even the wisest sage, can do anything about the years. They pass regardless of our efforts, wishes, and actions. Some throw in the towel, roll over, and take whatever the years choose to dispense without resistance. Some fight the years with external procedures, not all of them without merit.

Those on The Project take measures to make the years serve them, knowing their Paths provide the means for not only spiritual health but also physical health. They know that while the years will take a physical toll, they are determined the years will not take a spiritual toll.

Intellect

All education is self-education, whether the resources of a great university are utilized or whether someone chooses to educate themselves. Regardless of how it is done, we must make the most of it: a student who spends four years binge-drinking and taking notes probably hasn't done themselves a whole lot of good, just like the autodidact who seldom leaves the couch is not being of use to anyone, either.

Whether in a classroom or on our own, we must constantly educate ourselves because we need a persistent, working mind to discern the beneficial from the useless. An old saying about minds being like parachutes and working best when they are open is correct.

Sage

Anyone can be a sage after sufficient time on their Path because the years offer wisdom and context to all who are open to receiving them. Sages have no special skill; they have merely opened their minds to all possibilities and liberated it from all shackles. They realize past notions and habits could, will, be superseded in time and, while respectful of the past because it is the foundation for today, they remain open to the possibilities of the years because they know time will yield fresh prospects whether or not they are open to them. A sage is nothing more than someone who has left common concerns behind for an uncommon life.

Philosophy

Philosophy does not necessarily mean spending long hours pouring over words written 20 centuries ago that may or may not hold your interest, make sense, or have any practical value. Philosophy is nothing more than studying wisdom, and the only real wisdom comes from experience, and anyone can get that from being on their Path.

The longer you are on your Path, the less confusing outside influences become. Your actions and those of others and the randomness of daily life are immediately put into context. True separates from false, perception from reality. Your Path separates you from the common, allowing you to become yourself.

Dispassion

Time on your Path will teach you to view everything dispassionately. Does some success come your way? There is no reason to get too worked up; it was probably the result of planning and effort. Of knowing what you wanted, working for it diligently, and coming back strong from the inevitable setbacks that attend all achievement. You may also have felt the ultimate success was there for the taking, a trait common to some great people, both good and evil.

When an effort does not produce the desired end, introspection is in order. Was the plan workable and attainable? Was the effort true? Did everything come from the heart, or was it a reaction to outside forces? No matter the reason, you will withdraw all lessons for later use.

Limits

Limitations must be respected, and anything deserving of respect is good. When we know our limits, we know what we are capable of accomplishing. Those who make the most of their time on this planet work within that framework. They do not waste their time on the unattainable.

Definition

Those on The Project have simplified their life by reducing it to the one thing that matters: making their time serve them. They decline to mark time and squander their talents, preferring to march ahead on their Paths. Sometimes progress is slow because this is not a shortcut to the end of the rainbow, merely to the life you are meant to live. Sometimes, though, progress is swift and the results extraordinary, exactly what we dared to dream of. Either way, we have been liberated from the constructs and limits others continue to tolerate. The only slots we fit into are the ones we assign ourselves.

Tulips

Tulips are wonderful examples of The Way. They come when nature beckons in the spring. They bloom and spend their time fulfilling their purpose before returning to the ground.

So do we. With our first steps on our Paths, we are mere buds. In time, we learn what we are about. We blossom and fulfill our purpose. And like the tulip, there will come a time when we call it a day and go back into the ground, too.

This causes fear in some people, but The Way teaches us to embrace it because there is no reason for someone fulfilling their purpose to fear death. The tulip squanders neither time nor opportunity, and neither will you.

Blooming

One of life's great lessons – hard-earned in some cases – is that matters cannot be forced. Our lives must bloom naturally. When we do this, all things come to us and what is meant to happen in our lives tends to happen.

This does not mean we procrastinate, though. Procrastination is not on anyone's Path because it is merely putting your life off until tomorrow. It is laziness, ignorance, and fear of the imposters known as success and failure.

We must be patient and not lazy. Good things take time, and we must work our Paths with diligence and courage.

Idleness

It's OK to be idle. Both our minds and bodies need it because both can be overused and become weary. When this happens we are no longer making progress, we are merely marking time.

For some, idleness is an acquired trait, with some obliged to start with only a few minutes of downtime and steadily increasing from there. For others, it comes naturally. Either way, we must listen for and pay attention to the voice inside that says it is time for a break. Idleness is not procrastination, it is giving mind, body, and soul a needed rest.

Liberation

Losing interest in something that once completely occupied you can be confusing. However, if you turn it over confusion becomes liberation: one road has been walked and a road to fresh challenges appears.

It's a long life, and we cannot remain mired on mountains already summited. There are no anchorages on our Path, merely waypoints we pass and summits we climb on the way to our ultimate destination.

Direction

The need for direction is universal. For nature it begins with the sun. For us humans, it starts at birth and never ends. As kids we depend on our parents and as we get older others assert influence on us. As adults, external guidance is everywhere and those yearning to comply have no shortage of ways to do so: religion, many years of formal schooling, career paths.

Satiation and material accumulation, however, while offering some circumstantial solace, does not offer direction, merely wandering. Instead of traveling to the center of their being on their Path, wayward adults, lacking direction from their core and constantly reacting to events and people, never come close to living from the inside out.

Expectations

It is best to hold no expectations, a lesson it takes time to learn. This is because accomplishments are heralded every day to the extent some think wealth and notoriety are the only successes.

Nothing is further from the truth. When we are on our Path we naturally do the things we should be doing. What we do is irrelevant. The Way will show us what that should be. When we do those things, the success that comes from living the life you are meant to lead will be there waiting for you.

Question

Nowadays, it is common to question things, be they traditions or instructions or beliefs and it is right and proper to question The Way as well. After all, it requires an extraordinary amount of effort and commitment and everyone should know why this effort is worth their time.

The best way to question your life is go out and live it from the heart, to completely immerse yourself in your Path. Partial involvement will not work. You cannot follow your heart some days and not others, some years and not others. You must be on your Path every day, from the day you made the commitment until your day is done.

Being immersed in The Way answers the question why we are on our Path: because it allows, demands, us to march in step with our inner self. Once we are doing that, all questions about The Way cease.

Gifts

The Way bears gifts. There is the gift of daily progress, the realization of how differently you are handling events, others, and yourself even after a short time on your Path. There is the long-term gift of realizing how far you have come and how far you have left to go.

The road, for both novitiates and adepts, is not easy. People come and go. The imposters known as success and failure will rear their heads and we will dismiss them because our

Paths carry us past such petty concerns as whether or not others applauded or hissed at our efforts.

For those on their Paths, every step forward pays the dividend of knowing every facet of their being is being integrated into the whole that is their Path.

Responsibility

It's comforting to depend on people, of course. No one can go through this life completely alone. Even those who prefer to live without the commotion of daily companionship depend on their grocer and their barber.

When all is said and done, however, the only barrier between us and what we want to accomplish in this life looks us in the mirror every morning. If we are truly not happy with where we've been, where we are, and where we are going we have two options: we can whine about it or we can do something about it. We must not start by blaming others. First look inward, where the only question that matters awaits us: are we on our Path?

If you are on your Path and times are tough, that's OK. Your Path merely takes you where you are meant to go; it does not guarantee the end of the rainbow. Continued diligence and your Path will again guide you towards peace. If you've fallen off your Path, continued diligence will take you back.

Change

Not everyone adapts to change, be it changes around or inside them and it is not uncommon to run into people who are living the same lives they lived two or three decades ago. On the other hand, you may find you're living the life you were leading two weeks ago. This could be disconcerting to anyone living or wallowing in the past, but for you, it is merely further steps on your Path.

Knowledge

The only real knowledge comes from experience. Of course, we all need guidance, but until you've gone and followed your heart and trusted your instincts yourselves, until you've stepped out on your spiritual wire without a net and made it safely to the other side, until your Path is actual and not theoretical, knowledge of The Way will elude you.

In order to know, we have to do.

Morning

The morning is spiritual. The morning is renewal. Refreshed, we rise to face another 24 hours, a circumstance shared with every other human.

For both novitiates and adepts the morning is the time when we decide how we are going to spend our day. Whether we are going to put our time to work for us – and if so, how we are going to do it – or whether, and how, we are going to squander it. We must not wander aimlessly through the decades. A good life is dependent on good years and good years require a collection of good days, and a good day starts in the morning.

Afternoon

The afternoon is practical. While we can make the best of plans in the morning, those plans will not be any good if they aren't executed. We go from looking at ourselves in the morning to looking our Paths squarely in the eyes. When we do this, we see ourselves, of course, a person facing their day with determination and confidence.

As you gain time on your Path, you will find that your heart and your instincts will increasingly make decisions about how your day will be constructed. Your plan is made for you; all you have to do is execute it.

Forever

Forever is a long time, and despite everyone's best intentions, when it's time to part, it's time to part. There is no sense in banging your head against a wall trying to rekindle what was there, or what might never have been there in the first place. Sometimes we must go and sometimes the decision is mutual and sometimes it is made unilaterally.

The Way will make it clear when it is time to separate, and it is our duty to recognize when a particular cycle of our life is ending. When we do this, parting is easier. For those on The Project, the goal is to put nature and circumstance to work for them, and when either nature and/or circumstance dictate it is time to part, we must let go.

Solitude, whether voluntary or enforced, is a blessing. Leaving when it is time is liberating, freeing you from something that was neither working nor beneficial in exchange for a Path free of stagnation and encumbrances.

Destination

Ambition is an interesting animal. Of course, few things of substance are attained by accident. However, sometimes setting out to do specific things is limiting us to what we want to do instead of what we can do. This is a lesson that is hard-earned, even for those following The Way. We must accept that the harbor we are sailing toward might well be far off. This is showing patience to see our journey through to the very end.

Day 2

Some people approach any religion or spiritual discipline eager for a quick solution to their problems. And certainly, there are benefits to the optimism and joy that attend the start of the journey. Day 1, the day the decision to seek spiritual self-cultivation is made, is an important day.

Day 2, though, is even more important. It's the day you sit down and realize the challenge you have given yourself: a journey with an unknown future that doesn't end until you do. We see the enormity of the task we have set for ourselves and some, perhaps most, shrug and decide the price – daily attention to mind, body and soul – is greater than the price they are willing to pay.

Some steps forward on Day 2, however, make the following days easier. Soon enough, the perseverance required to turn days into months falls from us like leaves falling from a tree, and there is no going back to the days before Day 1.

Peace

The ultimate goal of any spiritual discipline is peace. A life at peace with nature, with ourselves and with others, at peace with the prospect of death. Some disciplines teach of a supreme being that offers everlasting life in exchange for some money and the following of some strictures, thereby liberating adherents from worrying about their time on this planet. A lot of, most, spiritual ways are dependent on adherence to external influences.

Some on their Paths dismiss these beliefs because they are dependent on elements that do not come from their inner self. Those on The Project reduce life to its most basic element: nature. They realize nature issued all of us assorted talents at birth and our best life comes when we spend our time maximizing those talents. Peace is achieved by focusing on the knowable and the doable.

Effortless

Everyone, even those squarely on their Path, has times when they feel a half-step off, when it seems you are watching your Path instead of walking it. Nothing you do is effortless; everything is a struggle. This is the time to do nothing because nothing is effortless, and when you are effortless, you are close to The Way.

When we let nothingness assert itself, we shut out outside influences and the longer we are effortless the easier nothingness becomes and the more in tune we become with what our heart is telling us. The tugging inside us gives way to peace. Struggle has yielded and the superfluous and unimportant have fled and we are content to be face to face with ourselves again.

Sharp, Quick, Determined

This is one of the benefits of The Way. It makes you sharp, quick, and determined because, after enough time on your Path, everything is automatic. You no longer have to think about steps you need to take to remain on your Path because you take them automatically. Your mind is completely focused on living the life you are meant to live and guides you accordingly.

And when something doesn't go quite right – as it sometimes, often, does not – you don't fret about it; you turn it over and make something good happen because time on your Path has shown there are few situations that cannot be turned to advantage.

Joy

Joy is the feeling – intrinsic and stemming from deep inside yourself – from knowing you are living your life and no one else's. You've exchanged the superfluous for the inherent, the gratuitous for the essential, the mindless for the substantive. It's a life that is there for everyone, but few seek it but once found, it is difficult to turn back from.

Inner Voice

You see this a lot here: every human being on this planet hears an inner voice. It is our obligation to not only hear them but also listen to them and act on them. Those working The Project listen to their hearts and follow their instincts because their hearts are telling them where to go, and their instincts are telling them how to get there.

This is what makes The Way so difficult: it is not easy to go against society's grain. There are an awful lot of people who have plans for us: spouses, friends, co-workers, and parents, among others, and it is human nature to want to get along and not disappoint. Consequently, an awful lot of people spend an awful lot of time complying with what others want them to do.

We must comply with ourselves. When we start answering our inner voice, soon we will know no other way.

Stretching

Some might interpret The Way as passive, merely going through life accepting what comes on the theory that what's meant to happen will happen without effort from us.

This is false. Our Paths take effort. Every day, from the day we accept the challenge until the day we die, we must stretch and strive for things we haven't attained before.

- Some things we strive for we will catch, life's great prize.
- Some things will elude us, life's great lesson.
- Some things we will chase until the day we die, life's great challenge.

Regardless of the result, those on their Paths have the wisdom to know what to strive for. They see the opportunities for stretching and striving they are presented and they take advantage of them.

COURAGE

...if one proceeds confidently in the direction of his dreams, and endeavors to live that life which he has imagined, he will meet with a success unexpected in common hours/If you have built your castles in the air, your work need not be lost; that is where they should be. Now put the foundations under them.
Henry David Thoreau
Walden

Wisdom is the necessary building block for courage because if we are courageously chasing the superfluous, we are wasting our time. Wisdom makes courage possible because when we know what we are about, it's easier to go and get what we want out of this life. Courage is not easy to muster, however, because we all know people who are not showing this courage, who are content to take whatever comes along and it is difficult to go against society's grain.

Difficult, but worth it.

Duty
There are joys to life, of course, but getting on is mainly getting up every morning and putting some work in. Work at spiritual self-cultivation, work at being you, work at transcending the pettiness and bickering that occupy others. This takes courage because so few people do it.

You will quickly become adept at bucking the norm; you will refuse to settle for anything less than the life you are meant to live. You will put the wisdom you've gained of yourself to do things you have a knack for: the things your heart is telling you to do. This is enjoyable, of course, but it is also solemn because now you must show the courage to be on your Path every day. You have a duty to yourself and the universe not to squander either your talents or your time on this planet.

Complexity

Simple people get simple results, and we all know people who decline to think outside their own small spheres. These people are nonadaptive, unimaginative, and, frankly, not particularly interesting. This is too bad because these people are not doing themselves or you and me any good. They are breathing our air, not utilizing time, merely marking it until their day is done.

It's a complex world so we must be complex, too. We have a responsibility to know ourselves, and this is why those on The Project remain on their Paths: because, slowly and surely, our Paths reveal ourselves to us. Others can hide behind tradition and precedent and hide from themselves, but you have committed to knowing every fiber of your being. Being complex means accepting everything your Path has for you, including faults and foibles. It is up to us to either surrender to them or show the courage required to conquer them.

Participation

We must participate in our lives, not merely watch it; our goal is not to overcome others, but to overcome ourselves. The work involved in trying to control nature and circumstance is as enormous as it is ultimately fruitless because nature and circumstance are there to be utilized, not conquered.

From the time we make the commitment to spiritual self-cultivation until we call it a day, we participate in nature, in the seasons, and in ourselves.

Promise

Different disciplines promise different things. Some promise a hard life of deprivation and want as a road to enlightenment. Some promise multiple existences. Some promise wonders beyond our life here.

The Project has one promise: the life you are meant to live. It's both easy and hard. Easy because all you will be doing are things you have a knack for and cultivating the talents you were born with. It's hard, though, because doing these things makes you different from most others, the others who have decided to ignore the dictates of their inner self. You have broken away from the herd to find a life that few others even bother to search for.

The seeker of spirituality is really seeking themselves, and The Project will ensure you find yourself every day. You will learn the discovery of yourself, the only discovery that matters.

Movement

The sand in an hourglass runs a straight course. It has no other options. It can't sneak outside and open a secret door to the bottom of the hourglass. It goes where it is told and does so with alacrity. There is no stalling, there is no waiting for the right moment to proceed, there is no rushing. The last grain of sand cannot get through the hourglass any quicker than nature intends. The sand simply goes when the hourglass is turned over, taking the exact amount of time that it should. When the sand is at the bottom of the hourglass, it waits – neither patiently nor anxiously – for its next movement.

Similarly, we follow our Path without waiting for a right moment that might never come. Like the sand, we can't rush our Paths, and when it is time to rest, we do so, waiting for our Path to figuratively turn our personal hourglass over for our next movement. When it does this, we simply go, just like the sand goes from the top bulb, through the neck to the bottom bulb.

Everything moves, including, especially, us and we must have the wisdom and the patience to understand their movements. Just like the sand, we squander neither time nor effort. The sand's only goal is to go where it is directed; our only goal is to go where our Paths direct us.

Time

The only time we have is now. What are we doing with it? Are we squandering it in mindless pursuits that yield no other dividend than having been entertained, or are we putting it to work for us? Even one second ago is a memory and the next hour can only await our entrance. We humans are experts at procrastinating. The diet will start tomorrow. That chair will be built tomorrow. The stone steps will be climbed tomorrow.

Those that get on in this life start today. Those following The Way know there is no better time than right now to show the courage to do what needs to be done.

Restraint

It's hard to be uninhibited, to live without restraint. From the moment of our birth, compliance is mandated, and while we might think adulthood might change that, in truth, even more compliance is required as a grown-up, by work, by family, by society.

Now, uninhibited in this context does not mean merely being impertinent. It means liberating ourselves from the constraints of human nature. It means declining to fit into slots assigned by others. It means overcoming ourselves. This is not always easy. All of us have an inner self that commands us to do things, but human nature does not instruct us to do those things. If it did, more people would do them. Most of a good life is breaking the restraints we impose on ourselves.

Complexity

Adherents realize they cannot be all things to all people, so they try to be all things to themselves. They do this by reducing their lives to a few things that matter. They determine what is important to them by listening to their inner self. They know there are a lot of people telling them a lot of things, and they've learned their inner self is the only voice that can drown out the cacophony of others.

The more others are drowned out, the more in tune we become with ourselves. Soon, there will be no more questions, only actions that come straight from our hearts. With diligence and courage, we follow our Path, not some days and not others, but every day and all the time. We are living the life we are meant to live without question and without compromise. We have become one with ourselves and have become us.

Mastery

We all have our talents, and using those talents leads to experiences and skill. If we stick with it, we are rewarded with mastery. This is one of life's great prizes because mastery leads to insights into ourselves and into other things, both others and circumstances. It doesn't matter what this mastery is in, either. Talents vary, and those who get on in this life utilize, maximize, and master theirs.

It's not easy to find mastery, though. It involves a journey to the very core of your being, a journey most choose not to take. You, however, have the courage to take this journey. The biggest obstacle to the life we want usually looks at us in the mirror every morning, and we must be committed to overcoming that obstacle.

Inner Self

There are a lot of spiritual paths out there and you may even have tried some of them. You will find that you remain on your Path because you see The Way removing all barriers to the very core of your being. You have found the wisdom offered by your inner self, and now you have found the courage to follow its commands. Others may follow the dictates offered by the myriad of supreme beings that have evolved over the centuries, but you follow your Path secure in the knowledge it is taking you exactly where you are meant to go. You are living the life you are meant to live, without compromise and without exception.

Artist

Adherents look at their lives like an artist looks at a project. The artist possesses both a long-term view of what the finished project will look like and the work that must be expended to make it happen. There is also self-confidence that they can make the project a success. Those on The Project know that if the artist is willing to put that much care into obtaining the desired result, then they can put no less care into their own time on this planet

Every day, The Way issues us a blank canvas, and we decide what goes on it. We can utilize our time and talents to put precise strokes on our canvas, or we can squander these resources and put scattered strokes on our canvas, or we can waste everyone's time and put nothing on it.

We must be committed to producing a worthwhile canvas every day. To do this, we must utilize the same courage, diligence and patience an artist utilizes. When we do this, the canvasses of our life will combine to produce a wonderful mosaic.

Money

The Way does not concern itself with the size of one's bank account. Some on their Path have a knack for making money, while some find their Path tends to provide the money they need.

Both too little and too much money can cause problems, and those of substantial means have the same problems everyone else has. Those on their Path of modest means might be broke, but they are never poor. Everyone on their Path has the wealth of the soul and the satisfaction of living the life they were put on this planet to live because there is not one necessity for the soul that can be purchased.

Perseverance

James 1:4 says – depending on the version of your Bible – "Perseverance must finish its work".

Perseverance in our spiritual lives is no different than perseverance in any other aspect of our existence: we must keep plugging away. Some days are easier than others in any endeavor, and those who quit on anything – artistic vision, personal goal, spiritual quest, it doesn't matter – take a pass on withdrawing every possible benefit from the experience, and they will probably quit on future endeavors, too.

We must finish what we start. Once we've started on our Path, we must show the perseverance to see it through to the very end, otherwise we are merely serving time while on this planet.

Instinct

We say this regularly here: the purpose of The Project is not to deliver the end of the rainbow; it's to force us to come to terms with what we are meant to do with our time and then spend our time doing just that. Everything – guidance from masters, readings, meditations – is either in support of or ancillary to that. We must have the wisdom to know ourselves, the courage to live the life we were put on this earth to live, and the patience to do this until our day is done.

When anyone wastes either time or talent, their instincts let them know because something inside them gnaws at them, telling them this is not what they are supposed to be doing. Some ignore this, but you are not. You have the courage to go against the grain of the herd, and you are liberated from the shackles of compliance with external forces.

Bravery

We must be brave if we are going to live the life we are meant to live.

Every day, circumstances can keep us off our Path. The car broke down. A project at work demands our time. Friends offer enticements and amusements, and it takes bravery to overcome our entirely human nature to settle for what's easiest. Others don't want us to try and accomplish things, probably because they themselves have never tried anything, preferring the comforts of inaction and conformity.

Those working The Project are brave, going through life with strength, power, and confidence. It is the strength that comes from knowing their purpose in life, the power from living it, and the confidence from the attainments that happen along the way.

Small

It pays to embrace the small. The pyramids weren't built from the top down and Mount Everest cannot be summited while wandering the Gobi Desert. Every step we take, especially small ones, is important, a building block of our pyramid. When we have enough blocks laid, enough steps taken, and enough courage and patience shown, then we will find ourselves at a summit.

Seeking
Life's great lesson is those who put work into their lives see results. Those who seek self-cultivation on their Path find the rewards of the soul. Those who react solely to outside influences, who ignore their inner self, will look back on time and talents squandered. Their time is not serving them; they are serving time while on this planet.

You will see progress every day, though at the outset progress may be hard to find. Sufficient progress, though, yields triumph over the temporary and the external, the petty and inconsequential, but mainly triumph over yourself. What were once obstacles now provide inertia. What were once hindrances have become inspiration. You have sought and found The Way and, therefore, have found yourself.

Burden
Our burden increases as the years pass. In youth, age and demise are as distant as they are abstract, though there will come a time when we realize we have lived far more days than we have left. The purpose of any spiritual discipline is to rid its adherents of a fear of death, and the only difference is in how each discipline goes about relieving this fear. Some offer prospects of eternal glory – or, alternately, damnation – in exchange for some beliefs and, as likely as not, some money.

Our only belief should be in ourselves. Rather than fretting over what may or may not lie beyond our existence here, we should put our time and talents to the greatest use. When we do this, our fears of leaving this planet are replaced by the satisfaction of having a life worth the effort we put into it.

The Road
The difference between success and failure in anything is generally hard work, and those who are willing to put in that work generally get the results they are looking for. Those who

decline to put in the required effort sometimes find themselves looking back at what might have been.

Our road is going to wind and the years are going to pass regardless. Spiritual self-cultivation might seem like a lot of work, but after time on your Path you will see the results of making your time serve you, of having taken the road less traveled, and you will look back and see it wasn't that much work at all: you had merely shed convention to maximize your talents and live the life you are meant to live. You will look back on time well spent.

Obligation

We are all issued 24 hours every day – the only commodity we all have in equal measure – and the first choice we make every morning is whether to use those 24 hours or waste them. Everything we get out of this life stems from this decision.

Some take this obligation seriously, while some disregard it. Some realize the work that will be involved and embrace it, while some see the work involved and turn away. Some see the patience required and embrace it, while others will decry the lack of more immediate results. Some embrace the responsibility of putting daily work into their lives, while some resist the lack of a deity to take that responsibility from them.

Expecting perfection is folly. We're humans, not images on stained glass windows, and everything we do is flawed. It's the way the world is built. We accept this obligation, and by doing so, we know and are ourselves.

Difficult vs. Easy

In theory, the initial decision for spiritual self-cultivation may seem easy, but when faced squarely, it is difficult because it means throwing away familiar, comfortable ways of living. Determining what you are about is difficult because it means squarely facing your inner self. Having the courage to live the life you are meant to live is difficult because it means breaking away from the herd for a road few others dare take. Eventually, though, your courage pays off, and your Path will become second nature. Ease will replace difficulty.

Today

The past and the future have as much influence over us as we let them. We cannot spend time fretting about or reveling in yesterday or worrying about tomorrow. One cannot be changed and the other cannot be scripted, only anticipated, waited for, and then pounced. Today is the culmination of our yesterdays and the first stone step to our summits of tomorrow. You must take advantage of every today.

Change

Some find this difficult to accept. One reason people pursue a spiritual quest is for stability, consistency, and regularity. The desire to avoid or mitigate change is a fundamental part of our human experience.

The Project offers these things but in entirely different contexts from what some are looking for. The stability comes not from ancient texts, but from the day-in, day-out journey on your Path. Consistency comes not from visiting a sanctuary every week, but from visiting your inner self every day. Regularity comes not from mindlessly passing days and years responding to external circumstances, but from being open to what nature and circumstance put in front of you, from making your time serve you, from making regular progress up the stone steps.

Accomplishment

Those who accomplish great things generally set out to do great things. They realize Everest cannot be conquered wandering around the Gobi Desert. This may seem like a contradiction because The Project teaches and demands that we free ourselves from ambition, but it's not. We are content to follow our hearts and trust our instincts because our hearts are telling us where to go and our instincts will tell us how to get there. Sometimes we are led to great things.

Great or small – like good and bad, success and failure – are mere imposters that exist only in relation to one another. Take one away and the other goes with it. We should only want attainments that stem from our inner self. When we do that, we can leave judgment to others.

Living

Some disciplines emphasize works or faith as the primary point of existence. Some, though certainly not all, of their adherents find this comforting: a spiritual minimum wage that offers the peace that comes from following a specific doctrine, a spiritual orderliness that takes the work out of living. You comply, and certain rewards are promised, though due to the nature of our existence, no one really knows if these promises are delivered.

After sufficient time working The Project, you will not bother fretting about what happens after death because you are eagerly putting work into the *right now* of your own life. As you get on in this life, you will both look back on and ahead to time well spent because every day is another block on your pyramid.

Conflict

Our times are not unique: our planet is a war-torn, savage mess now and has been since time immemorial. Followers of The Way tend to disdain and avoid conflict because that which is in conflict is not in harmony, either with nature or with oneself.

When faced with conflict, we must first look inward and ask ourselves if we are at fault, either through ignorance or error. If so, we make amends. If the conflict was caused by others, we take whatever action on our end that will eliminate the conflict, generally something passive that will remove us from the conflict. This could mean either no longer doing certain things or dealing with certain people, both of which can be difficult. If the conflict demands confrontation, then we are committed to strength because sometimes the only way to eliminate conflict is to do something immediately and for good.

Regardless of the cause of the conflict, we aim to return to our Path as soon as it is practical.

Interference

We do not interfere. We do not tolerate interference in our lives and do not offer it to others.

More than interfering with other people or things, though, we do not interfere with ourselves. We get out of our own way and eliminate the indecision, laziness, procrastination, and fear that attend every life and are not necessarily reserved for novitiates because those with many years on their Path fight them, too.

We work every day to stay out of our own way. Every morning we wake up and reaffirm our commitment to spiritual self-cultivation because we do not want barriers or interference. We've come this far and there is no point in turning back. We do not interfere with either others or ourselves.

Questions

When the time comes to evaluate our lives, we will realize that the only big question is whether we are happy or not. Did we do well? Are we looking back at time well spent, or are we looking back at talents wasted and time squandered?

It's good to question. Those that do not question do not live. Those who do not question accept the very least life has to offer, wandering mindlessly from day to day until one day they wake up wondering what might have been.

Those on The Project live knowing exactly what they are about, regardless of where their Path takes them. They question themselves daily: are they on their Path? Is there time serving them? Are they touching the very core of their being on a daily basis? They remain committed to answering yes every day.

Worthiness

We talk a lot here about how success and failure exist only in relation to one another: take one away, and the other disappears, too. All we are left with is the work we put into something. When that effort is true, it is a worthy accomplishment regardless of the results.

Those on The Project aim to be worthy of themselves. They know their deeds – great or small – come from their heart, directed by the inner self that has taken command of their lives. By definition, their lives are worthy.

Discipline

We all face the same blank canvas a painter faces. The painter knows what he wants to create and takes the time to execute his vision. So do you, without compromise and, after some time on your Path, even without instruction. Every day both adherents and the painter show the discipline required to put their hearts and souls into their canvases.

Cultivation

A cherry tree was born to be a cherry tree. It does not fritter away its time trying to be a rose bush. Similarly, we should not bother to be something we are not. We were born with talents and interests, and those who get on in this life spend their time cultivating those talents and interests.

These talents may or may not interest others. They may or may not cause us to live down the ages. It doesn't matter. Like a tree grows and takes advantage of what nature and circumstance provide, so, too, do those following The Way. Like the cherry tree, they are determined to cultivate everything nature has given them.

Repression

We must not repress ourselves. We must, selflessly and selfishly, use our Paths to our own ends. The only way to look back on a life well spent is by expressing ourselves, by letting every talent bloom and flourish, by living and not merely existing. When we do this, we will have good days, and those good days will lead to good weeks, months, and years. When our day is done, we will look back at a life well spent.

Education

The very best education is knowing yourself. Those who spend their time in mindless revels and provide knee-jerk reactions to outside influences miss out on knowing the most important person in their lives. We are the only person we see every day, and those who go through life not knowing their inner self are missing out on life's great prize. When the time comes to examine their lives, they find themselves looking back at what might have been, life's great tragedy.

The journey to our core never ends and, in time, when you examine your life you will find there are no what-ifs because you have maximized both time and talents. You will look yourself in the eye and say you did well.

Conformity

Those with time on their Path reject the conformity mandated by others. Revels, pastimes, and customs treasured by some are waved aside by those on their Path. For those following The Way, the only conformity is with their inner self, their core, their soul. Others can wander on defined trails while you will wander in the undefinable and end up exactly where you are meant to go.

Acceptance

Does acknowledging the impossibility of perfection mean we are settling? Of course not. Those working The Project do not settle, but they do accept. They accept the imperfections that attend everyone, even, especially, someone on their Path. They accept both their talents and their shortcomings. They use the years to provide the context that turns lessons into experience and wisdom.

Depth

Those on any spiritual journey are looking for something more than daily selfishness. Some are content with finding a way around our utterly natural fear of death, while others seek a structure for good works, thought, or scholarship.

Those following The Way demand more. Yes, they are looking to overcome everyday fears and lead worthwhile lives, but more than anything, they are looking to transcend everyday life and reach the very depths of their souls.

It's not easy. It requires daily work, diligence, and courage. But when someone has reached this depth, nothing can challenge, obstruct, or deny them. They will do what they are meant to do with their lives regardless of who applauds or hisses.

Connection

True spirituality in any discipline involves a complete connection with something greater than yourself. For some, this means a connection with external sources: sacred texts, ancient ways, mystic spirits.

You are doing the opposite. You have disconnected from the external and are connecting with your inner self. You embrace the daily journey on your Path because everything else is superfluous. By reducing your life to a few things that matter, you are liberated from the compliance required by others and are free to become your own peg in your own slot.

Ease

The only thing worthwhile in this life that is easy is sleep, and even that's hard sometimes. Everything else takes work, be it physical, intellectual, or spiritual. It is even difficult to quit, because here, too, you must overcome yourself by turning your back on both yourself and work previously put in.

Life on your Path is not easy. It requires enormous self-awareness and commitment, daily self-cultivation, and extraordinary patience. While not a lonely Path, it is solitary, as people see they do not have the desired influence over you, stand back and sigh, and leave your realm. Others, though, see this commitment and are drawn towards you.

Unseen

The unseen can be difficult, seemingly impossible, to relate to and this difficulty is handled differently by people and spiritual disciplines. In religion, the unseen requires faith. For followers of The Way, it merely requires acceptance.

Those following The Way tend to ignore unfathomable things or things for which they cannot provide answers or explanations. There is no way to know with certainty what happened before our planet was formed, so we accept that we may never know.

They do know, however, that their time on this planet is finite and of unknown duration and we must be determined to maximize our time here and not fret over the unknowable.

Poetry

Not everyone has a poet's knack, just like not everyone can repair a car, teach a class, or lead a group. Sometimes, the poet's analogy is more figurative than literal. It's difficult to write lines of a certain meter that rhyme and mean something, and it is best left to those with the skill and energy for this work.

We all have something inside us, though, a figurative poem waiting to be written. Every single one of us can do something well. Those who get on in this life have taken the time to determine what this is, and they spend their time doing these things, doing them regardless of the fortune or notoriety they may or may not bring. They do this merely because this is what contents their hearts.

The Way shows us that the very best subject for a poem is our own life, with each day inscribing another line. We can either write a new line each day or we can leave the page blank.

Zenith

As we've discussed from time to time, you do not spend your entire life on the summit. Eventually, you must return to base camp and get on with daily living, at least until the next summit presents itself. At the pinnacle, we must be careful not to get too full of ourselves because success and failure have both been dismissed as irrelevant. All that matters is we set a goal, worked to make that goal happen, and saw our efforts rewarded. It is important to remember most of life is lived on an even keel, and every peak is followed by an inevitable valley. It's the way the world is built.

Immersion

Those who find The Way find it can be a demanding master. Oaths, creeds, or sacraments used in the past have no influence here; they will only get in the way because their new place has completely rejected the place they came from. If you are going to succeed in your new place, you must immerse yourself totally. It's like swimming: you must dive in for the full experience.

The Way is no different. It requires complete immersion. You must be on your Path every day. Not some days and not others, not some weeks and not others. The journey must be made every day, every week, and every year, from the time you make the commitment until the day you die. There is no middle ground. Either a woman is pregnant, or she is not, and either you are on your Path, or you are not. In time, this will become automatic. At first, it takes thought, diligence, and complete immersion.

Accomplishment

One of life's great lessons is there is generally someone better than you. Now, there are some that reach the pinnacle, where they look back and see everyone and look ahead and see no one, but this is rare.

Some do not take this well. Renown is what they are looking for in life, and when they do not get enough, or even any, it sets them back. Those on their Path, however, have long ago realized they are nothing special, merely someone trying to get on in this life, someone trying to make something good happen for themselves.

Realizing there are people ahead of you can be discouraging or it can be liberating because you are free from trying to reach subjective standards set by others.

When you have met the challenges that attend becoming your very best, you have proven yourself to yourself, and once we have done that, what else is there to know?

Diligence
Humility is ideal, but The Way allows for you to be pleased with things you've done: you followed your Path with diligence and courage until you reached your goal and you have every reason to be pleased. There were no guarantees you would make it and it was entirely possible the goal might have eluded you. There might be a billion Chinese who, as the saying goes, couldn't care less about your attainment, but it was important to you, and you climbed the mountain, and at these moments, no one can pull the summit out from under you.

Hard earned and well done.

You must not, however, rest on your laurels. One of the joys of this life is fresh prospects, and after an appropriate time, your Path will carry you on to other things. These are to be embraced because today's accomplishments merely lay the foundation for future successes. Yesterday cannot be grasped, it can only be learned from as you move from one summit to another.

Abandonment
Some might think that abandoning ambition means you are giving up on accomplishing something. Nothing is further from the truth.

Those who have set aside ambition have merely set aside the imposters that are success and failure. They have dismissed material goals for self-cultivation. They are content to pursue something by merely using their cunning, intellect, and ability without regard for the outcome. Liberated from external constraints, their inner force is now their ultimate power.

Destiny
Followers of The Way know their destiny comes from inside rather than from the mystical, that dividends derived from their time on this planet stem from the work they put into their lives. By and large – and to an extent that astonishes some – they get out of their lives what they put into them.

Now, it's important to note adherents are no different than anyone else: they do not know what their destiny is any more than you do: they only know that by following their Paths they will get there eventually; adherents know that while you cannot dictate your destiny, you can prepare for it.

What destiny are we preparing for? Are we preparing for a destiny that is a product of walking our Paths with diligence and courage? Or is our destiny going to be a result of ignorance, of not getting to know ourselves, of spending our time reacting to outside influences, of fitting into the slots assigned by others? Will we reach the summit of Everest or will we choose to wander around the Gobi Desert?

Difficulty
Nothing on this planet has an easy life. Predators are prey themselves. The rich have the same problems as the poor; they can only purchase better help and may eventually realize there are no material solutions to spiritual problems. The

beautiful and famous are exploited so the masses can be entertained. Those with average measures of things find they must work to make their time serve them, too.

It's useful to watch the animals we disturb while conducting our lives. The ants we pester while working in the yard go right back to work immediately following our disruption. They don't stand and stare at us, and they don't wonder what to do next, and they don't form a committee to look into the matter: their instincts send them right back to their assigned tasks. We must be the same: regardless of the disruption or the difficulty, we immediately go back to our Paths.

Reflection

We should look for The Way everywhere. In ourselves, of course, but also in others and in our surroundings because only by looking for The Way will we find it. We should especially look for it at the end of the day.

We must have the courage to ask, did we make the day serve us when we could? Did we show compassion, patience, and wisdom when needed? Were we true to our inner self? Were we of service to ourselves and others? Finally, mindful that good lives are built on good years and good days, did we lay a good foundation for tomorrow, or did we squander today?

Understanding

The only real understanding is that of ourselves, and a profound level of awareness is why any adherent stays on a spiritual path: they are looking for something more than the superfluous cares and activities of everyday life. Whether it's an organized religion, a pagan discipline, or The Way, those involved are looking for something deeper than daily selfishness.

The only way to achieve the profound is to chase it on a daily basis, and this is the biggest challenge of self-cultivation. Our Paths are there every day; they do not take a day off and neither can we: a day of supposed leisure and respite from your Path leads to two such days and the next thing anyone knows a week has been frittered away and before long we are telling ourselves we will resume our Paths tomorrow. Then tomorrow never comes and The Way is in the rearview mirror, traded in for mere pleasure, and those who waver will never know how close they came to the profoundness they were looking for.

Clarity
Few things of substance happen by accident. We say this regularly here: you do not climb Mount Everest wandering around the Gobi Desert. Most great things are attained because someone dares to be great.

Now, that doesn't mean we can set out to do the impossible. Not only must the goal be clear, it must be attainable, too. That is why you seldom see adherents practicing to earn spots on the Olympic sprint team: few have that ability. While we must follow our hearts and trust our instincts, we must expend our efforts on things we have a knack for. We must not bang our heads against the wall.

Followers of The Way know this and focus on goals that are attainable. They don't fret over subjective goals or try to clear hurdles set by others. They know they set the only bar that matters, that of their own existence, and they know great results happen when the goal is clear.

Creativity
Many of us have some sort of creative bent. The problem is that we are force-fed examples of people who have turned their creative bent into fame and fortune, which establishes

– and later reinforces – the idea that fame and fortune are the only worthwhile rewards. Nothing is further from the truth.

This is why adherents stick to their Paths every day. They know that by living from the inside out anything produced by the heart and soul is splendid. Every living thing is capable of something wonderful; all we have to do is dare to find it and dare to be great when we do find it.

Flame

Like water, fire is a common metaphor for Tao. A fire starts out from a spark and becomes a flame and then, sometimes, an inferno, before ultimately being extinguished. This is akin to the human experience, where we start small and grow. Like a fire, we are here only for an indeterminate period of time.

Those who get on this world find their flame and stoke it on a daily basis. When this happens, we become a flame that is not extinguished until our day is done.

Curiosity

Curiosity should never diminish. It does, of course, leaving those who no longer welcome it, those who have become content with the frivolous and superfluous, with the mindless passing of the years. With all dreams and ambitions successfully squelched, they are waiting for the end to come and get them, instead of charging to their finish line with strength and purpose.

We cannot discourage ourselves because the road seems long, nor can we let others discourage us simply because we do not fit into their assigned slots. Our Paths satisfy our curiosity, assure our individuality, and maximize our initiative, ensuring that every day, we are taking steps, sometimes leaps, forward instead of merely marking time.

Progress

Anything of substance requires daily work. Champion athletes may take a day off from training, but even rest is a planned element of their regiment. Some reading into Michelangelo's painting of the Sistine Chapel shows a man completely consumed with his task, weary with his enormous labors, but desirous of seeing it through to the end.

Mortals like us can be no less consumed with following our Path. While our lives and accomplishments may or may not live down the ages, we must be completely consumed with the task of painting the canvas of our lives. Even a day off of our Path, a day spent chasing frivolity and the superfluous, can mean missed progress and opportunity. When we leave our Paths, the beauty of progress stops.

Altars

An altar can be many things.

Those with experience in a sanctuary are familiar with large and elaborate altars, and it might be interesting to note that some modern churches – mostly non-denominational and more casual than some traditional worshipers might feel comfortable with – do not have altars at all.

Individual altars vary greatly, as they should because no two Paths are the same. Generally, a personal altar will be where we do our daily meditation. It can be as elaborate as a sanctuary's altar, with statues and incense and candles, or it can be as simple as the desk, table, or bookshelf where you keep this book. It can be anywhere because The Way is everywhere. Our altar provides a spiritual center point, a place we can go in times either turbulence or calm to reinforce our spiritual efforts.

Disengage

It is necessary to sit still regularly because only when we are alone with our thoughts can we refill our mental tanks. Just like our bodies can't go indefinitely without rest, neither can our minds.

Like everything else in life, people disengage differently. Some are able to sit quietly and empty their minds of everything. They sit and focus solely on a single point in their mind, and they have the patience to do this for extended periods. They save activity and engagement for when their bodies are active and engaged, thereby achieving the rare state when all elements are running on all cylinders.

Others find that when they are sitting still their minds go into overdrive, immediately offering fresh prospects and inspiration. This is good, too, because only when the mind is freed from obligations imposed by the body and others can it be completely liberated.

Wayward

Some people drift mindlessly with the breeze. They have neither a destination for their lives, nor a course charted to take them there. They respond to this outside influence and that external force and are like birds in a windstorm: they are blown here and there, never arriving at where nature intended them to go. When their time comes to die, they wonder what if.

You will find few what-ifs on your Path because you are doing the things your heart commands you to do. Your Path is taking you to the very core of your being, and you happily take this journey to the very end.

Here And Now

Courage

We must have the courage to live in the here and now because it is the only time we can make serve us. Yesterday is gone and was either productive or squandered. Tomorrow, as the song says, is always a day away.

We cannot fret over yesterday or events from long ago – though we will learn from them – because they know a productive here and now lays the foundation for productive tomorrows, while a squandered here and now creates more distance for us to cover in the future.

Essence

Those working The Project find laws are few, but they are exacting: search yourself so you have the wisdom to know what you are about and the life you are meant to live. Show the courage to go and live this life. Do this every day until the day you die. When we do this we are completely in step with both the spiritual and practical traditions of The Way and have found the essence of ourselves.

Self

Following your Path is both selfish and selfless. Selfish because we have decided we have one shot at this life, and we are not going to waste it fitting into slots assigned by others: we will do things our way and will blaze our own trail. On the other hand, time on our Paths is completely selfless because being of the most use to ourselves is the only way we are going to be of any use to anyone else. The Way is a course to the very center of our beings. When we've arrived, we have found ourselves and will do the right things intuitively.

Engagement

Worse than marching out of step with events is marching out of step with yourself. We have all had that gnawing feeling in our gut telling us this is not what we are supposed to be doing right now. It can be something as trivial as merely wasting some moments of a day or as momentous as embarking on a life step we know we should not be taking, like an ill-advised marriage or career change. This gnawing shows we are not engaging ourselves; it is our inner auto-pilot trying to keep us on course.

Those not on their Paths dismiss their autopilot, passing on opportunities to engage their inner self. In due course, we will not only recognize our autopilots, but we will act on them, engaging ourselves and our lives every day.

Focus

It's hard to focus on many things at once. There are vocations and avocations to pursue, families to raise, and other demands, too. With our focus on so many things, sometimes we end up scattered emotionally and physically, and there isn't enough left to look after ourselves.

This is why adherents tend to stick with The Way once they've found it: their Paths give them a focal point for their time on this planet: your only obligation is to complete your own journey. We are relieved from scrambling to comply with the dictates of anything but those of our inner selves.

Natural

Animals follow their instincts as a matter of course. Without question and every day. When it is time to fly, birds fly. They don't consider the matter and file a flight plan. When there is nothing to do, animals rest.

We humans are different, though, and we do not always follow our instincts. Instead, we question them. They tell us to go and do something and we do something else. Friends and family have expectations for us and those are sometimes difficult to ignore. Every day we are bombarded by outside influences vying for our attention, a myriad of obstacles to overcome. Overcoming these obstacles, however, liberates us to follow our instincts as naturally as a cat sits in the sun.

Experience

We humans consistently meet the expectations we have for ourselves. Those who accept negativity and mediocrity soon find they have taken root. Those who expect good things generally find that, after appropriate planning and effort, they were there for the taking all along.

We cannot do anything about the years. There were billions of them before us, and there are billions more to come. But we can do something about the years we have, and we will get out of this life what we put into it. We must expect nothing more from our time on this planet and demand nothing less.

Obstacle

We do not need to lead a tactical life however, like a warrior, we must be ready. Every day, there are dozens of distractions that can lure us off our path: amusements, obligations hastily made, people requiring compliance we are not prepared to offer, the list can be never-ending if we let it. Proof that we are our own biggest obstacle can be found in the fact there is no shortage of people who will start something tomorrow, a list that might well include us.

Followers of The Way do not allow this to happen: they take everything and everyone as a potential obstacle to their Path. They realize their only obligation on this planet is to complete their own journey, and they jealously guard their Path against any element that can cause a distraction. Every person and situation is immediately – and, after time, automatically – evaluated; in time you will only admit those who will accent your journey without obstructing it.

Rules

Human nature dictates we have a structured society and it has mandated this since forty-five centuries before Christ. It's the way the world is built.

The Way has rules, too, and they are very clear: our Paths must be followed every day. Not some days and not others, not when it is convenient or comfortable. When we do this, we not only follow The Way's rules, but our own: we are in step with the natural order and ourselves. We are following the only rules that matter.

Serenity

Serenity can come at any time and can disappear as quickly. True, anyone from adepts to novitiates can find tranquility in being still, but a warrior may find tranquility in battle, while a conductor or choir director may find it in the midst of the brilliance his or her charges are producing. Everyone finds it when they are doing what they are meant to be doing.

Wheel

When the cart's wheels stop turning, the cart stops moving forward. So it is with us. We must always be in harmony with ourselves and move with nature. Like nature moves seamlessly from one season to another, so must we always keep our wheels turning and move seamlessly from one cycle to another.

Limits

All of us are limited. There are even limits to what our Paths can do for us. It cannot guarantee wealth or notoriety or even specific attainments.

But some of our limits are self-imposed. Fear, doubt, and the utterly human need to belong attend everyone. Those who get on in this world overcome these traits and themselves. While we are limited by the resources nature gave us, we have both the need and an obligation to reach those limits.

Because where there are limits, there is also liberation.

Released from having to meet the limits imposed by others, we are freed to reach our own limits. Freed from the shackles of ambition, we are liberated to achieve what we are able to, rather than what we want to. The Way allows us to withdraw every possible benefit from this life. We meet our potential, but we avoid attempting more than we are capable of.

Devotion

You can take all the swimming lessons you want, but until you actually go into the deep end without your instructor and your floaties, you really aren't swimming.

Similarly, you can read about this spiritual path or that religion, but until you actually put instructions into practice you've merely acquired some knowledge.

It's easy to be devoted when things are going well. The challenge is adherence and loyalty, constancy and allegiance, when things are a half-step off. This is when it is vital we remain on our Paths: the devotion that led to previous summits will take us there again.

Doing

When some were young, they dreamt of doing things. Then responsibility sets in and some dreams fall by the wayside and are not pursued. Few sadder words exist.

Those working The Project do the things they dream of. They are determined that the above words will not apply to them. When their time comes to die, they are determined to look back on having done, on having accomplished, on having followed their heart.

Adversity

It is human nature to look elsewhere to explain misfortune. But it is important to ask "Did I do anything to cause this?" and to give ourselves an honest answer. If we did contribute, or even cause, something untenable, we must make amends and do what is required to ensure it does not happen again. If it wasn't our fault, it is generally unconstructive to assign blame or to expect an apology and, here too, it is useful to what is required to ensure it doesn't happen again. This could range from making a note to identify and avoid certain situations in the future to even dismissing certain people or experiences from our lives.

Fear

There are, if we allow them, a lot of fears to face: fears of failure and success, fears of disappointing or alienating others by not conforming to what they want us to do. Fears of the unknown coming from ditching the familiar for spiritual self-cultivation. But unless we are facing an animal with bared fangs or some impending natural disaster, our only fear should be the fear of being off our Path

Fear can prevent us from recognizing fulfillment because it blinds us to what really is. When this happens, we miss recognizing when every possible benefit has been withdrawn from a situation. When we dismiss fear and its imposters, we are liberated to be content with the past while being free to pursue the future.

Certainty

Conforming to nature and not others is what sets you apart. Nature created The Way and nature issued everyone assorted talents at birth. We create our faith – in The Way and our Path, but mainly in ourselves – when we spend our time maximizing and utilizing these talents. It is the only way of ensuring a life well spent, a life of benefit to yourself and others.

While there are no guarantees in this life, there is certainty. The certainty of our hearts and our instincts. The certainty of 24 hours every day and the certainty of The Way taking you where you are meant to go.

Inside

Every good thing in our lives stems from something inside us. Usually, this is subtle. It's like dawn or dusk, a gradual change.

Your decision to work The Project came from the inside. You have shown the wisdom to know what you are about and you are showing the courage to turn words you are reading into the life you are living. Your focus has turned inward, your journey the focus now and not the instruction you are receiving. We all need guidance – even masters have masters – but in time, you will realize that while The Way is everywhere, it has, from the start, been deep inside you.

Roots

There is enormous strength in being on your Path. People and events that would have once influenced you no longer do because you have put some things behind you. Events, to a degree that can be astonishing, go your way. You are living life on your terms and don't think others don't notice. They can only sigh at the lack of control they now have over you.

The fundamentals of The Way never change. It is us that changes as our roots in our Paths take hold, allowing us to bloom.

Holy

Holiness is relative. Some disciplines offer a supreme being as an example of holiness. You are learning that holiness comes from the inside. Living in concert with The Way has given you clear recognition of the true nature of life: that you have a finite amount of time on this planet, you had no control over when it began and almost as much control over when it will end.

Holiness comes when we control the time in between our beginning and end. Those following The Way know when their time comes to die, they are going to ask themselves if their time yielded dividends for themselves and others, or whether it was squandered. It is the only question that matters, and we must answer it in the affirmative.

Imagination

As kids, we all went to bed at night dreaming of doing things. Now, we may no longer have these dreams, either because we chased them and either caught them or they eluded us, or they were never chased at all. Dreams can change, too, because we humans change as well.

Those following The Way know their Path is nothing more than their imagination focused on a desired end. We long ago decided to chase our desired ends, and it doesn't matter what the desired end is, either, because all of us have different talents and goals. What is sacred to some might bore others.

Those who get on in this life turn their imagination into reality. They pursue their desired end.

Home

It's good to get away from home from time to time. It's refreshing to give our minds an airing and it really doesn't matter where we went or what we did. Simply being out of the familiar puts our minds to work, preparing us for new insights.

Some simply are not content at home. This is not ideal. We must be comfortable in our own homes, just like we must be comfortable in our own skin. Those who are never at home are not giving themselves the opportunity to be themselves.

Heart
There is always the commotion of outside influences demanding our attention. Those we know say this and want us to do that, some of it worthy of our attention while some of it are merely attempts to get us to fit into the slots they've assigned us. These are challenging to ignore and difficult to refuse.

Followers of The Way, though, regularly ignore and dismiss the regulations imposed by others because they know the only truth is spoken by the heart. When it's time to act, it's time to act, even if that action is merely standing by and letting matters go on without our interference. Our hearts and our Paths will reaffirm us daily if we let them.

Progress
Great athletes did not become great by training every few days. They trained every day, even if the day's training called for rest. Similarly, great lives – lives that are useful to us and those around us – require similar effort. We must be relentless in making our time serve us, and our inner selves will let us know if we have made progress or marked time.

It is important to note that daily progress does not have to be great; it only has to be steady because life is a series of steps and not a succession of leaps. Satisfactory daily progress over sufficient time will yield great progress, and in due course, a new you will show itself in the mirror.

Strength

Those following The Way are mentally strong. Now, when you are first starting on your Path, you might have to force yourself to be mentally strong. You might spend no small amount of time deciding what you should be doing and how you should be doing it. This is normal. After all, you are taking the first steps on a journey that demands complete focus and unyielding determination, and mental strength and clarity must be earned.

As we've noted, however, once you spend some time on your Path, your connection to The Way strengthens, and you move forward confidently and without second thought. Your time on your Path has ensured that your mind will not give way.

Guidance

Guidance at the beginning of any endeavor is invaluable. It gets you underway with confidence and provides stability when in doubt. It keeps you focused on the desired end even when the desired end may not be clear. But it is not a crutch, and you cannot depend on it forever, only as long as necessary, much like training wheels are shed in due course.

Independence comes not when you can live without being on your Path but when you possess complete and instant recognition of your Path, when you are so in tune with where your heart is telling you to go you head there as a matter of course, utterly without thought. You are on your Path, and your Path is now your guidance.

Apex

Every experience eventually has a time when it has shown everything it has for us. Either a good situation has had every possible benefit withdrawn from it, or it is time to exit a bad situation. The key is to be in tune with yourself so you can recognize these instances and, perhaps, even see them coming some time beforehand.

This is not always easy. It's difficult to let go of excellence and the joy of accomplishment can sometimes overcome the clarity of your instincts telling you it's time for something new. Similarly, you can become so immersed in something unproductive you can't look up and see your way out.

Followers of The Way do not have this problem. They recognize an ending cycle when they see one and they know this liberates them to move toward the next one.

What If

From time to time we all run into people who say they should have done this or they should have done that when they were younger. Sad words because they refer to years and sometimes decades wasted, never to be retrieved. You must be determined to say this as little as possible – if at all. We must go and do the things our inner self commands us to do. We may not be young anymore, but this is a gift because the years give us wisdom and context. As time passes, you will find you are not looking back on what might have been, you are looking at what is.

Alone

It's not easy to go it alone, but whether we do or not, we must be capable of it. This doesn't mean we shun others or remain a closed book to them because people need people, and adherents are no different.

However, while people come and go, our inner selves remain constant. Those on The Project ask for nothing more than life on their Path but they also demand nothing less, attracting and repelling people over the course of a life. Through the momentous and the mundane, we must have the courage to be good company for ourselves.

Core

Those not on their Paths sometimes fight themselves. They're brains go into overdrive over things you dismiss as petty, unimportant, or trivial. Besieged by outside influences, they wonder if they are reaching the yardsticks put up by others.

Those on their Paths do not have this problem. They dodge the yardsticks others have put up because they realize they do not accurately measure their lives. The only waypoints to be acknowledged are those set by your heart. This usually comes in the form of inner satisfaction from having done what you were meant to do.

Your core is sound, and so is your life.

Zenith And Nadir

The sun rises to its zenith and then begins to set. So it is in life. We rise, and we wane, and the funny thing is, we may not know when or where our zenith might be. We might think we do. We might think one accomplishment is the salt and summit of our existence, but what do we know? Everything in existence is transitory.

This is the beautiful thing about being on your Path: you do not know what it has in store for you. Sure, one accomplishment is nice, but there might be others waiting for us. Zenith and nadirs are merely aspects of our lives, not ends in and of themselves.

Celibacy

It is important to note that celibacy – whether self-imposed or enforced by others – is part of our Path. It's not always easy because our marching orders from Mother Nature are to reproduce. That is all she cares about. She really doesn't care about our Paths or making our time serve us or anything else except men and women procreating.

Sex, of course, is natural and part of The Way, and our Paths will tell us when to be celibate and when to take advantage of what interest and opportunity present to us. We must be careful, though, because while a wanted child is a Path's richest blessing, an unwanted child is a burden.

Solitary

Every adherent is on their Path because they were not satisfied with the ordinary and made a commitment to self-cultivation. They had no interest in taking roads commonly traveled. They are determined to avoid serving time while on this planet; they will make their time serve them.

The decision to embark on spiritual self-cultivation is so solitary even our Paths take a non-committal attitude. It's there for us, for everyone, but it has no role in our deciding to follow it. It merely awaits our decision.

Beauty

While following our Paths is challenging, it is merely what Nature wants us to do: take full advantage of what it has in store for us. This includes both big-picture opportunities and small things that might well be forgotten the next day. When we stop and appreciate a flower or a sunset, we are not only appreciating this small token of beauty nature has given us, but we are also taking time to appreciate ourselves on our journey.

Interaction

To ignore the world is to ignore ourselves. We've talked about the billions of people on this planet all leading random lives, and we are included in that: we never know which way a course goes until we follow it, and we may never know when our random lives will influence or benefit someone.

Our Paths are our ultimate nourishment, but we must be active participants. Our Paths do not follow us; we follow our Path.

Circumstances

When adherents are unable to attempt or accomplish something because of circumstances out of their control, they usually find their Paths provide a way around the obstruction. When something not to their advantage happens, they turn it over and make something good happen. They expect good things and others are sometimes surprised at how often adherents get good things that, perhaps, they themselves wanted.

Strength

Those on The Program are mentally strong and the key to a strong mind is focus. We must have the focus to be completely in step with our Path.

We can't put our Paths off until tomorrow. We can't be on our Paths some days and not others, some weeks and not others, some years and not others. We must have the strength to be on our Paths every day from the time we make the commitment until the day we die. That is the only way we are going to live the lives we were meant to lead, the only way to allow what is meant to happen in our lives to happen.

We have two options: we can yield to the vision others have for us or surrender to the vision our hearts have for us. Surrendering and letting our minds focus on our Paths takes courage, but displaying this courage allows us to live the life we were meant to lead, with some finding it was there for the taking all along.

PATIENCE

Perseverance must finish its work.
James 1:4

Patience is the anchor of a well-lived life; however, it is completely useless without Wisdom and Courage because if you lack these two elements, you are merely waiting.

Finishing
While talents and interests differ, we all have 24 hours every day, the only commodity all of us are issued in equal measure. What we get out of this life depends on the work we put into those 24 hours. Those who get on in this life maximize their time and talents. Those who are left wondering might have been generally squandered their time and talents.

The Way liberates us from fretting about the usefulness of our lives. Whether we are exerting concerted effort or resting, whether we are being of service to ourselves or others, we must be committed to making every one of our 24 hours yield a dividend. You've started your Path and patience allows you to stay on it.

Frivolity
Frivolity versus substance is a battle fought every day. It doesn't end merely because you are on your Path. All working The Project means is you have determined to put in the work required to live the life you are meant to live.

Each one of us faces the same battles every day: the battle of living from the inside out, the battle between work and ease, the battle between frivolity and substance. The battle awaits us every morning when we wake up, and when we look ourselves in the mirror, we must decide whether to fight it or surrender to it.

Work

The difference between looking back on time well spent and looking back at time squandered is mainly hard work. It is not the type of work that builds pyramids or fortunes but the work that determines the life you will lead and whether or not you have the patience to do that work every day.

All of us have things we must do in this life. Most ignore them or, perhaps, try them and quit at the first reverses or challenges. If you made it this far, you are doing the things you must do every day, without apology or compromise. Your mind is focused on doing your work every day.

Renouncing

Spirituality involves a lot of renunciation, be it a philosophy, another spiritual discipline, or organized religion. Adherents are asked to give up something, and it's usually something we like.

You are now renouncing everything that doesn't matter – everything outside your inner self, the unnecessary, the temptation of the easy, and the trivial. When you renounce the unnecessary, your life is reduced to the one thing that matters: the life you are meant to live. You started this journey with tentative steps, but now you are confidently on your Path, and you will be until your day is done.

Time

Our lives are real and far from illusory, but they are transitory. There are things we may borrow until we die, but we don't own anything because everything carries on once we're gone. Those who get on in this life realize, accept, and even thrive in the passing nature of life. They know the years provide context and insight and that everything can produce dividends. We remain on our Paths so we can withdraw these dividends.

Habit

We humans are creatures of habit, guardians of our routine, and interpretations and perceptions formed early on continue to steer us in later years. This is both good and bad, depending on the habit or perception, with established habits capable of producing either inspiration or restraint.

Knowing their Path won't squander their time, those on The Project realize that everything and everyone they come across can yield a dividend. Time on their Path has shown them how to disregard the templates of habit that used to govern their lives.

Uninhibitedness

The opposite of uninhibitedness is stagnation, and adherents decline to stagnate even though every day offers 70 times seven opportunities to do just that. Our actions are sure because they come from deep inside, fresh because our Paths regularly show us new prospects, and creative because no one else is us. We each have our mandate, and when we answer to this and live the mandate from our hearts, we create ourselves every day.

By declining restraint and embracing our inner self, we are uninhibited in pursuing our Paths. Our engagement with the life we are meant to lead is total and complete.

Relativity

An empty house is a blessing for some and is sad for others. A great deal of money is useful for some, a curse for others. A lion in a cage poses no particular threat unless we are in the cage with it.

The only thing that is not relative is time: the 24 hours of each day and the 365 days of each year that are there for everyone. It takes courage to grab hold of those 24 hours and put them to work for us, and it takes patience to do it every day and every year. It also takes courage to turn your back on those 24 hours, to stifle your inner self, and to squander your time by measuring up to the standards others set for you and not the standards you've ser for yourself.

The hours and days are not relative; they are there for all of us to face each day.

Fate

All of us have lives we are meant to live. While our circumstances vary, the only intrinsic difference between us is some live that life and some do not. Fate is what awaits us when time and talent have either been maximized or squandered.

This is not a fate worked out by a mystical force; it is the fate borne out by the work we've put into our lives. It is the fate earned by either answering to or ignoring our inner self.

Now, specific results are not known in advance: it could be a life that lives down the ages or a life that barely resonates outside our front door. Either way, it's a life useful and pleasing to adherents and useful to those they come into contact with. It is a life spent mastering and overcoming ourselves.

Elusiveness

There are times when The Way can seem enormous, elusive, and unknowable. Whether novitiate or veteran, it is normal to see the enormity in both nature and our collective human existence and wonder where our place is and, when we find it, to wonder if it means anything.

The Way keeps it simple, allowing us to block out external forces and pin ourselves down, a wonderful dividend of peace and confidence. When we follow our hearts and trust our instincts, we are no longer elusive to ourselves. We are squarely on our Paths, our time serving us instead of merely marking time. After some years, you will see patience has done its work, and we are looking back on and forward to time well spent.

Immersion
Our Paths are not something that can be walked in our spare time. Those who spend only part of their time on any spiritual quest generally end up disillusioned because their part-time results do not produce full-time benefits.

Any spiritual endeavor must completely consume its adherents. Those new to The Way quickly learn the quest for their Path must take complete hold over them and that wisdom, courage, and patience must all be equally present. The wisdom to know what we are about will do us some zero good if we don't have the courage to go where our inner self tells us to go, and courage won't do us any good if we don't know where we are going and patience is useless without its two partners. Only when we have completely immersed ourselves in The Way will the life we are meant to live unfold.

Resting
Rest has not always been easy to take. Since time immemorial, people have always had the need to go, move, and do, usually out of necessity. As humans advanced and invented devices that were supposedly going to make our lives easier,

we found we were busier than ever. There is always something to do, be it a task or an amusement, something productive or something mindless.

We must be keen to spot appropriate times to rest because – as a car will eventually run out of fuel – so too will the mind, body, and soul if not properly rejuvenated. Even a short amount of time on your Path will show the importance of rest. Adherents take advantage of these opportunities in the same way they take advantage of opportunities to go and make something good happen for themselves.

Structure
There is structure at the start of any spiritual discipline. A new religious convert reads sacred texts, memorizes creeds, and learns specific rituals. A Buddhist might sit still for hours, quietly intoning to themselves. A Taoist will look inward.

Regardless of the discipline, in due course, creeds are learned, enlightenment realized, and one's Path made clear. Instead of plodding along your spiritual Path, your Path is now second nature, the stone steps ascended without thought to the steps, the work done as a matter of course.

When this happens, you are completely in tune with your inner self and all obstacles between you and the life you are meant to live have been removed. You and your Path have become and will remain one.

Peace
Opinions are like fingers: everyone has a few. This is especially true about us: others have opinions based on what they seem to know about us. This is our reputation.

Those on The Project don't worry about their reputations because they know that life on their Path is who they really are. This is our character and can differ from what others think. This bothers some, but we shouldn't care either way: we do what we are meant to do with our lives and let others do the same. While others draw whatever conclusions they want about us, we are at peace with ourselves and the world.

Mastery

We will always be a work in progress. We must accept this and eagerly absorb the context and wisdom the years offer because it is the only way to go from the desert to the summit. The only benefit stagnation offers is the comfort of the familiar.

There are lessons every day. Mastery comes from heeding these lessons. Time squandered comes from ignoring them.

Imagination

Imagination is both easy and hard. It's easy to sit back and imagine things with little chance of happening. It is more difficult to imagine things that can happen for us and turn these images into a plan.

The decisiveness we showed in choosing to follow our Path brings wonderful dividends of control: control over our reaction to outside influences, control over how we choose to utilize our time, and control over what we choose to be important and not important to us.

Once we've established what we can and will control, imagination follows, leading to the confidence to show the patience to `remain on our Path until the very end.

Achievement

There is a saying in some circles that art is long and time is fleeting. This could cause some to throw their hands up and despair of ever trying anything, but those following The Way turn this to advantage. They realize their death is a foregone conclusion, so they don't worry about it. They focus on what they can do rather than fret over what cannot or will not be done.

Whether it's a life that lives down the ages or only brings contentment over having mastered themselves, your life will be one of achievement.

Labels

The closer we are to The Way, the closer we are to ourselves. This means fewer labels in our lives because imposters like success and failure can only stand back and watch because they have no power over us.

Labels are merely attempts to hinder us, so we must avoid those who try to label us. We will let others worry about labels, allowing them the privilege of fitting into the slots assigned by others. The only label we accept is the one we've assigned ourselves – someone on their Path.

Cycles

Life is a series of cycles and, like the years, they come and go. Those who get on in this life are adept at recognizing when cycles begin and end. Just like it is unproductive to continue a cycle that has run its course, it does no good to ignore the start of a new cycle.

One of the benefits of following The Way is being completely in tune with each cycle in your life. When it is time to part, it is time to part. When you have lost interest in something – even something you've long dreamt of – you are liberated to find something new. When a fortuitous or enjoyable circumstance has passed, it is time to let it go. This is not always easy, but a rearview mirror is only useful on a car. We must always look forward, the past winds for our sails and not anchors.

Retirement

Patience

As the years come and go, some retire, both from earning a living and from living itself. Their day is already done; they are merely marking time until nature makes it official.

You will never retire. As the years come and go, your Path continues to do the work we assigned it on Day 1. It liberates us from reacting to outside influences, allowing us to maximize our time and talents so that when our time does come, we are looking back at time well spent instead of time squandered.

Eventually, of course, our Path will take us to the very end, but only because nature and circumstance have determined it is time for us to go. It will not be because we have retired from life.

Balance

Upheaval occurs in nature and in individual lives, too. As we note here from time to time, our Paths do not take us to the end of the rainbow or offer shelter from misfortune and maladies. They merely offer a way for us to maximize our time, to live and die with no regrets.

Just like nature balances itself, so does our Path provide balance for us. Winter's snow is balanced by spring's thaw. The routine tempers exhilaration. Pain is balanced by time and renewal.

Most days are good, but some are very good while some seem beyond tolerance. That's OK; nature's balance ensures that all things eventually pass.

Change

Things change, of course, and we must embrace them. It shows that things are moving forward, either because inertia is pushing them or because someone has grabbed the bull by the horns and is changing them. When we resist these changes, we stifle our own growth.

Just because we've changed doesn't mean old temptations disappear. As they say in 12-step program rooms, your disease is out there doing pushups. The temptation could be a person or anything else that has caused problems in the past, like a habit that was never particularly useful.

But time on our Paths brings wonderful dividends. The problems remain the same, but we have not. Our transformation has vaulted us past the routine and superfluous cares that occupy others.

Two Decades

For those new to The Way, 20 years down the road could seem like a long time. For those who have 20 years on their Path, it does seem like a long time because they are looking back at a different form of themselves. They have gone – figuratively and sometimes literally – from wandering the desert to attempting to summit the mountain. They look back at a different person and look forward to the person another 20 years will produce. The transformation never ends, so we carry on, certain tomorrow's results will be worth today's efforts

Influence

Some time on your Path will likely show that it is best not to look to influence others. To force The Way is unseemly. However, a humble and thoughtful life will create a person who some will note, and adherents must not live in a shell. When required, they must share The Way with anyone they think will benefit, perhaps someone they see a reflection of themselves in. When this happens, it is appropriate to share. The humility, self-cultivation, and work that keeps you on your Path will allow you to share the way with others.

Looking Back

When our time comes to die we will look back on our lives and ask if we did well. Some will answer affirmatively while some, perhaps most, will be obliged to shake their heads and admit they did not do well. They will look back on squandered years, time served instead of time serving them.

In time, you will see the work you've put into constructing your life was really no work at all: all you've done is wake up every morning and try to maximize your time and the talents you were born with. You trusted your heart to tell you where to go and your instincts to show you how to get there. You are not wondering what if because you tried and you know.

Stillness

When stillness is absent, access to our Path is blocked. Stimulation and distraction only lead to a mind going in many different directions, a mind unable to focus. Stillness is not easy because the world never ceases to provide distractions and demands on our time. Those who get on in this life can say no to things that will prevent them from making their time serve them.

Those on The Project do not have special powers or magic touches that allow them to seemingly disregard external forces. They have merely put the years to work for them and in doing so, they have mastered and overcome themselves – life's great prize.

Engagement

We all have something inside us that commands us to engage with life. Some face this and shy away because they fear looking themselves in the heart.

This is not easy. It takes wisdom, courage, and patience – and no small measures of all three. It takes wisdom to read your inner force correctly, courage to go and live the life it is commanding you to lead, and patience to do this until the very end.

You must engage yourself every day. You have made the decision not to live on the sidelines, and you are realizing that your Path is the only way to completely engage your life. You have made the commitment to making life happen for you and not to you.

Learning

We try to learn. We go to schools and follow masters in an attempt to gain knowledge. The Way, though, shows that the only way to learn is for us to go out and live our lives and that our only real understanding comes from this experience. We can read about this and we can read about that, we can read about the splendors of making our time serve us and the wonders of serving our inner selves, but until we've actually gone and done these things it is not knowledge, merely a scrap of information we've accumulated. Information does not become knowledge until we've put it to use in our own lives.

Equinox

The changing of the seasons is nature personified. At the equinoxes day and night are roughly the same length, and the solstices herald the longest and shortest days of the year.

Our lives should be nature personified, too. We do this by not wasting time on things we have neither aptitude for nor interest in, instead focusing on maximizing the talents we were issued at birth. When we commit to doing this every day, we will enjoy a collection of good days, which will yield good years, good decades, and a good life.

Heaven

Patience

The concept of heaven is ancient. It might go by different names and purposes, but since time immemorial us humans have always had a concept of paradise outside of our earthly bounds. We needed it then, and we need it now.

Heaven is where you choose to look for it. Liberated from having to fret over an afterlife, those following The Way can find their own entrance to the bridge between heaven and earth. They find the entrance by following the dictates of their soul. They know the length of their time on this planet is finite with an unknown end date, and they seek to make every day count because this is how you make the years and the decades count.

Persistence

The time at our summits might last only minutes and times in the depths pass, too. When it seems we've stagnated or our Path has presented barriers, we must be patient and persistent. Patient because it is best not to offer a hasty reaction to a situation. Persistent because we must remain on our Paths regardless of whatever temporary circumstances happen to be presenting themselves. Our Paths will ensure our course is eventually righted.

Receptiveness

Most of being on your Path is being open to it. At first, many people may seem receptive to a spiritual life, but most flee when they see actual work involved, work that takes courage to start and patience to see through to the very end. They were receptive to the concept but not the practice.

Adherents are receptive to everything. They are receptive to looking inside themselves to find out what they are about, and each day they are receptive to where their time and talents will take them. At night, they are receptive to – and perhaps even demanding of – asking themselves how The Way manifested itself. They are receptive to what tomorrow will bring, though they may not be entirely sure what that might be. As their day ends, they find this receptiveness has led to peace.

Perfection
Perfection is not possible. In the context of us humans doing anything whatsoever, imperfection is presumed. Sure, judges might pass out perfect scores, and games and amusements might acknowledge certain results as perfection, but we humans are flawed, so, literally by definition, is everything we do.

We can, however, come as close to perfection as possible. Now, our Paths will not issue a gilded cage to live in, spare us from all discomfort, or exempt us from the usual human foibles and emotions that cause error and, sometimes, offense. We near perfection when we spend a day on our Path. When we do this, good weeks, months, and years follow. At the appropriate time, we look back on a well-lived life. This is as close to perfection as we can get.

Misery
People say this and people say that but no matter how often pledges and claims are made, little of substance ever changes. People do this and people do that but progress is slight, if noticed at all. Wars have been fought since time immemorial, with the only dividend generally being more war. There have always been haves and have-nots.

It is important to note that while everyone is born with talents, not everyone has the same opportunity to utilize and maximize them. Some are born into situations – poverty, warfare, repression – where they are not given this chance. Every day is a scramble, and survival is never a given. The talk of the splendors and wonders of spiritual self-cultivation would go in one ear and out the other simply because circumstances make the journey to their Path supremely difficult. This is lamentable, of course, and the world would be a better place if everyone had the chance to follow their Path.

Those who can't find their Path are no different from those who won't, so those who follow The Way are grateful for the opportunities others may not have and, therefore, never waver from their Path.

Death

Death has been the focal point of every spiritual discipline since time immemorial. The earliest practices involved ancestor worship and the arrival of spring was heralded – with appropriate human sacrifices – as a renewal of life. These were, perhaps, the seeds of life-after-death beliefs.

The Project is no different: it helps adherents come to peace with their own deaths. However, you are not chasing an afterlife, reincarnation, or eternal splendors; you are chasing a worthwhile time on this planet, a life that can be examined and judged to have been lived well. At the appropriate time, you will know you have made your time and talents serve you. What was meant to happen in your life has happened and there are no regrets.

Body

As we do good things for our soul, so, too, must we do good things for our body. So we try to eat well and exercise so we reap their benefits, both externally and internally.

Some take this literally. They realize that food is merely fuel to keep our bodies running and only eat what is required to keep their bodies humming on all cylinders. Others take a less literal approach, realizing there is nothing wrong with enjoying a fine meal, just like they enjoy other nice things in life. Both avoid the extremes of too little and too much food, just like they avoid the extremes of too little and too much exercise.

Starting or maintaining a spiritual quest with a body that always demands attention is difficult. A strong and healthy body is just as important to life on your Path as a healthy and strong spiritual life. Those following The Way have allowed their inner self to take command of their lives, and when they've done that, good diet and exercise habits tend to establish themselves.

Fantasy

We all fantasize. Fame, fortune, fulfillment, wanting all of those things are human nature. This leads to delusion because all fantasy stems from external sources: we see something we are told is desirable, and we want it.

Some learn the lesson that possession does not equal happiness, but many more do not. Some find the more they have the more they want and that no accumulation is ever satisfactory. They are locked in chains – sometimes made of gold – of their own making.

Those following The Way fantasize less and less as the years pass because they are completely in tune with what they are meant to do. They see no point in frittering away their time by going against their grain. While some, at the appropriate time, are looking back on delusion and decades squandered, patience will ensure you will look back on time well spent – the ultimate fantasy.

Concentration

We do not need to keep our noses to the grindstone every waking moment. Some leisure is needed for everyone. However, those who get on in this life do the things that are important to them, and they do them every day.

And it doesn't matter what those endeavors are, either. Some build chairs and some build companies and some direct choirs and what's important to you might bore someone else.

All of us can do something well, and all of us have 24 hours every day, the only commodity each of us is issued in equal measure. Those who spend their time doing what's important to them are the ones who can look at themselves in the mirror every morning because they are doing what they are meant to do with their time. Everything good – good days, good years, good decades – stems from the concentration required to do that.

Distraction

A good life requires daily cultivation. Just like the farmer cannot merely throw seeds into the ground, ignore them, and expect a good harvest, we cannot proceed aimlessly through our days and expect to satisfy a yearning soul. When push comes to shove, our only two options are putting daily work into our lives or frittering away our time on this planet and looking back at what might have been.

Repetition

The Project is not easy. It cannot be blown off in times of difficulty or inconvenience and utilized at need. We must have the courage and the patience to be on our Paths every day, from the time we decide to find out exactly what we are about until the day we die. Some days on our Path and some days off our Path do not do anyone any good whatsoever. It results in a haphazard life with little direction and few satisfactions of the soul.

Following The Way is an act that is repeated every day. While the challenge might seem daunting at first, in time, repetition makes it second nature; endurance yields custom, and custom yields the life you are meant to live.

Creation

Creating ourselves is our only real responsibility on this planet. We can create something useful for ourselves and others or squander our time on this planet by ignoring our inner selves and continually answering to outside influences.

Throughout The Project, we've noted the proverbial blank canvases we are issued every day and at the end of the day we look back on that canvas and ask ourselves did we do well or was our time wasted? Did we create a canvas that shows grace, direction, and precision, or did we create a canvas utterly lacking in harmony and structure? I can't answer that for you and you can't answer it for me. Only we can create ourselves.

Journey

Guidance can only take you so far. It can take you to the Path and even encourage the first tentative steps, but it can't take the journey for you. Adherents of all disciplines read sacred texts and search for examples, but that only scratches the surface. Regardless of the discipline, we must get involved to withdraw every possible benefit.

The methods vary. Those following an organized religion read ancient books, listen to sermons, and give offerings, but true belief only comes after going forth and actually living the lessons learned. Some will withdraw and live an ascetic life.

And so it is here. You can read this five times, but if you never leave your chair or start your journey, you will never derive the benefits that come from truly being on your Path. It is similar to an iceberg: the tip is merely an introduction, with most of the iceberg lying beneath the surface. Our lives begin beneath the surface, deep in the core of our being.

Dispassion

Patience

The highest highs and the lowest lows spark feelings and emotions that do not come around every day and The Way does not teach squashing these emotions. Emotions must be felt because to deny them causes them to fester and like anything that festers, eventually it will cause more damage than the original feeling.

And time on your Path does not make you unfeeling. Those following The Way feel the same exhilarations and sorrows others do, however years, sometimes many years, on their Path has changed how it affects them. We are all part of something infinite, and while we assign meaning to earthly things, nature does not. We are given time on this planet, and how to spend that time is the only real decision we have to make. Everything flows and expands from that. Time on your Path does not change your feelings, it merely structures how we react to them. It brings poise and self-assurance; eventually, you will find yourself keeping a calm exterior regardless of circumstance.

Equinox

The seasons do not change on a dime, they change gradually. The same is true on our Paths. Some days there might be noticeable, perhaps even significant progress, but most days our progress is imperceptible because it takes time to accomplish anything of substance. And there may be times when progress toward what we want seems slow or perhaps even non-existent.

Times like this present a crossroads for everyone. Those not completely focused on their goals might find they deviate from their original course. This is too bad because those who dismiss their goals will never know how close they came to reaching them.

You must be completely focused – not so much on a specific goal as on remaining on your Path. A mariner, after all, does not sail for a new destination when a storm blows them off course. No, mariners fix their position and chart a new course to the same destination.

Progress may be slow, but it will be noticeable over time. One day we try something and, after some time merely plodding along, we find we're better than we used to be or, perhaps, we've reached a summit.

Spectator

A banality is that life is not a spectator sport. Common, but true. There are those, though, who choose to view their lives instead of taking part in them. Long ago they chose to ignore the instructions of their inner self and take whatever circumstance gave them. They are spectators of their lives, watching the years pass. When the time comes to examine their life, they find they have no satisfactions of the heart and are left wondering what if. Their only accomplishment is getting old and, perhaps, holding on to a marriage that long ago lost its luster.

This is not what our human experience is about. Of course, we have Mother Nature's mandate to reproduce, but we also have the mandate of our inner self to go and do things consistent with the talents we were issued at birth. When we do that, we're participants in our lives and not merely spectators.

Misconception

Those who think that a new spiritual discipline will bring everlasting happiness are mistaken. No church nor temple nor Path makes every moment splendid. Even the hermit who has tossed aside everyone and everything but himself will have his campfire extinguished by rain. Those who have been on their Paths for decades also have their share of rain.

But those on their Paths know happiness every day. They are living the life they are meant to live, with neither time nor talents squandered. They withdraw every possible benefit from their existence, and this overcomes daily trials and tribulations.

Clarity
Few things are accomplished by anyone without a unified mind. The scattered mind never accomplishes much because it can never focus on anything long enough to see substantive results. People start something but lose interest when they realize the enormous work involved or when something shiny and new distracts them.

Those on The Project have complete clarity. They live life from the heart and have the patience to do this every day. They know that when perseverance is combined with the 24 hours we all have, clarity follows.

Barrier
Anytime we seek something specific, be it a gain or an advantage, we limit ourselves to what we want instead of what we can achieve. No one knows what they are truly capable of, and specific goals can constrain us. If we were to set out on an endeavor without specific goals and merely to maximize our talents and withdraw every possible benefit from an experience, we might very well find ourselves exceeding what we thought possible.

This does not mean adherents sit on their haunches and meekly accept what happens to them. Nothing is further from the truth. Ambition must be properly focused, and followers of The Way choose to focus their ambition on maximizing their time and talents. They know the results that come from that transcend success and failure and lead to the very core of their being.

Appearances

Those not on their Paths sometimes mistake pleasure, comfort, and being satiated with happiness. It's easy to do. We see pleasure and perceived satisfaction every day. We see others with nicer possessions than we have. Sometimes we seem to be bombarded with such examples and it's human nature to desire these things and to want a comfortable life.

This, however, is merely the appearance of happiness. No external element can buy one satisfaction of the soul, and all of us have purchased some item or experience only to find that after it is acquired, it is met with a shrug and wondering if that's all there is.

Followers of The Way know the only attainment is the abandonment of appearances and facades, of turning away from external influences, exchanging them for the satisfactions and attainments of the soul.

Sleep

Barring some physical malady, most followers of The Way sleep well. They are on their Path and consequently know good rest is time as well spent as the good hours they had during the day. They look forward to entering the absolute void and, perhaps, dreaming vividly.

If something troubling occurs in their lives, they determine whether or not they have control over it. If so, they have determined to take care of it with alacrity and tenacity and will sleep well. If they don't have control, they know there is little they can do and will generally sleep well, too.

A good rest is merely another part of The Way, as important as the other hours of the day.

Expectations

To a degree that surprises some, we humans tend to get out of this life what we expect to get out of it. Those who continually say disparaging things – about events, others, and even themselves – have few positive experiences because nothing measures up. Those who are content to wander from day-to-day squander both time and talent. Those who expect to come in second never win. The analogies and metaphors are endless.

Followers of The Way know this and remain committed to seeing the good in everything.

All things measure up, some in full measure, some in lesser measure, but the wise learn that very few situations cannot be turned to advantage and that there are benefits to be withdrawn from virtually every experience. We learn that what is merely another day of the same thing for some can be exciting, uncharted waters for those seeking self-cultivation. Adherents expect good, talk about good, and, as such, generally get good things.

Opponents

There are numerous opponents that can keep us off our path, and they are always outside our door doing pushups. They are myriad: procrastination, laziness, and fears of success and failure, to include some. While it becomes easier as the years progress, that doesn't mean the obstacles disappear. They don't. They are always there; all it takes is one lazy day ignoring your Path to turn the tide. Because while good days lead to good years and decades, so does one bad day lead to bad weeks and years and before you know it, a Path is a distant memory.

Rhythm

Those with more money than most sometimes find that a burden. They have what a lot of others want, and there are still questions that are unanswered because your Path cannot be purchased; it must be found and explored. Those who wander through life content to be entertained usually find themselves wondering if that is all there is because they've done nothing to ignite their inner self and have squashed all initiative, development, and success.

Each of us determines the rhythm of our life. No drum must go unplayed, and each of us has an obligation to tap out our own rhythm.

Blooming

Generally, The Way will guide us to where we should live. However, circumstances sometimes preclude this. We can't all flee to a beach or a village or the center of some industry. Perhaps this is because a loved one needs our attention or simply because it is impractical.

This is of no consequence because those working The Project know their Paths – along with general human adaptability – will allow them to bloom where they are planted. Anyone who follows The Way with diligence and courage will flourish wherever they happen to be. Our Paths ensure we are always in the right place.

Restraint

It is said, not without some truth, that those who threaten and bully are afraid, perhaps of their own weakness. Those who wield anger, jealousy, and vindictiveness are using these emotions as weapons as surely as a ruffian wields a club or a knife. The adherent realizes these are not constructive emotions and associate with these people as little as possible, ideally withdrawing from the interaction if at all practical.

Of course, there are times when we must assert ourselves. Wrongs must be righted, and the innocent must be stood up for. Regardless of whether their blade is their intellect, physical strength, or even withdrawal, we must be careful to use only the assertion required for success. The years teach that excessive displays of authority and power only cause resentment and further problems.

Cycles

Daily life is nothing more than the changing of the seasons occurring on a daily basis. Yesterday we were on our way to today. Tomorrow we start a new phase. Each day is different: we are a bit wiser and a bit more experienced than we were yesterday, so of course, today will be different. We will have insights we could not possibly have had in the past and that will lead to experiences we haven't had before.

We can't, however, fixate on either yesterday or tomorrow because today is the only day we can look ourselves in the mirror. We must look ourselves in the eyes and ask if we are doing well or squandering our time on this planet.

Death

The primary goal of any spiritual discipline is easing the fear of death. Dealing with death started in the earliest civilizations, where rites and rituals designed to honor the dead evolved into religion, and those adept at remembering and administering those rites and rituals in time became the clergy and priesthood.

The difference is in how they go about easing death's sting. Some teach that preparation for an afterlife takes precedence over any other aspect of life.

The Way shows and allows us to face death courageously. It shows that the only reality is what we have today, and we prefer to exchange the prospects of building for the beyond for the obligations of making today's time serve us.

Extreme

The Way shows us both good fortune and bad and we must avoid getting too worked up about either. Our Paths are all-encompassing and a variety of experiences await us.

This does not mean we are immune to feelings; however, we enjoy the good feelings that accompany accomplishment and attainment with the same equanimity with which we bear life's occasional sorrows.

However, it is important to note that good and bad exist only in relation to one another. In time, you will be able to dismiss both and let your life unfold, avoiding the extremes that hamstring others.

Voyage

Water is a good metaphor for a variety of reasons. One of them is that our lives are akin to voyages. We set out with a destination in mind and set a course for it, absorbing fair winds and following seas as well as the occasional tempest. The captain keeps his ship on course, righting his ship as needed during the voyage.

Through it all, the captain keeps his current position plotted on his chart. Whether using ancient or modern means, the captain always knows where he is and where he is going.

We will not reach a distant shore by merely casting off and waiting for the wind to blow somewhere. Far shores will only be reached by knowing where they are and setting a course directly for them. The ultimate destination may well be far off, so we must be prepared for a long voyage.

Narrowing
It's normal, of course, to think of our deaths. After all, it's going to happen. Perhaps soon, perhaps in many years, and unless we plan on doing it ourselves or have a death warrant signed by the governor, we don't know when it will be.

When we're young, we seldom think of our death. Why should we? Unless tragedy strikes, it's many years off. Our time is broad. That time narrows until we realize we've lived more days than we have left. This is one reason we think of and spend time with those who are dying, in the hopes others will do it for us.

All spiritual disciplines offer freedom from the fear of death and the narrowing of time. The only difference is the road offered. Religious adherents, offered the prospect of eternal life, live for the hereafter. Belief offers heaven, a hardened heart offers hell. The Way doesn't bother with what happens after we're dead; we walk our Paths until it narrows to the point where there is nowhere left to go.

Cultivation
All times of the day can be beneficial for self-cultivation. The morning, high noon, twilight—it doesn't matter; people are different, and various times of the day resonate differently with everyone.

What matters is finding a time when you can gather some time to yourself. The Way is always present and will provide benefits whether you use it as a springboard to face your day, a midday spark to keep going, or a way to wind down. This is the time to consider the lessons your Path had for you today and plan how to use them tomorrow.

The good thing about following your Path is you are completely in tune with nature and yourself and you don't need to spend time fretting over which time of day is best for you. The right time will present itself automatically.

Reward

Following The Way is always rewarding, leading us to times in our lives when we are completely in touch with the deepest elements of ourselves. It could be at the culmination of a long journey, where planning and effort have resulted in a desired outcome or it could come in the middle of an activity – either spontaneous or long worked toward – where every talent is being put to good use and there is a feeling of complete oneness with ourselves and the universe.

These are the peaks of our lives – just like the bad times are the valleys – and they do not come about every day. However, when they do, they are fondly remembered and the impetus for future accomplishments. It's when The Way has completely overtaken us, when body and mind – not to mention others – can only stand back and watch us triumphantly on our Path.

Assertion

Reading history is useful, and planning for the future is essential, but our lives are the only frames of reference we have. Our world exists because we are in it, living, moving, creating, and doing. Our ancestors had their time, and the future belongs to others. Our time is now.

Some squander their time, shrugging, ignoring their inner voice, and settling for mere existence. They follow roads commonly traveled instead of blazing their own trails. Eventually, decades have passed and they are looking at a body and mind well past their primes, the dreams and ambitions all of us were born with long ago abandoned.

Those on The Project must assert themselves while on this planet. They don't need to wonder where their talents, skills, and ambitions have gone because they are put to use every day.

Insight
Days and years following The Way give us the flexibility to realize things do not always go our way. As noted here, there are billions of people on this planet, all leading random lives, and sometimes those random lives affect us, just like our random life affects others. This flexibility leads to insights on when to assert ourselves and when it is best to let matters pass and run their course. All of this allows us to accept the fact that not even our Paths lead to the end of the rainbow. They merely lead to a well-lived life.

Nature
Circumstantially, The Way is for everyone. The Way, after all, is nature, and nature is for everyone. All The Way asks is that you be true to your inner self. The Way teaches that dreams are meant to be chased, not set aside.

Intrinsically, however, The Way is for very few for the same reason: following your heart and trusting your instincts can be supremely difficult. It requires stepping away from the herd and taking roads less traveled, difficult because this is contrary to human nature, everlasting proof that our biggest battle in getting on in this life is usually with ourselves.

Mastery
The Project isn't long division. We can't write it on a whiteboard so you can take notes and memorize it for a test. Sure, we can show you The Way and provide guidance and context, but you must reach the peaks and valleys on your own. And once your Path is found, we can't push you on it: you must climb the stone steps yourself.

The Way is the ultimate example of self-education and it's an education that continues until your day is done. You cannot walk someone else's Path, and no one can walk yours. You must follow your own. When you do this, you achieve mastery. You have become your own sword, sharpened on the steel of The Way.

Interval
Rick Wallenda, from the famous tightrope walking family, once said, "Life is being on the wire. Everything else is just waiting". It's a quote that cuts right to the heart of our human experience.

We all occupy our own wires, times resulting from much planning and long work, times that command the very best we can muster. These times could be known well in advance or could happen unexpectedly and could last anywhere from mere moments to days to perhaps even longer.

But these are not everyday events, and a good part of life is spent in the interval waiting for our wires to appear. The interval is good because otherwise the wonderful would become commonplace. Some, however, do not have the patience for the interval and chase the feeling that attends being on the wire through petty amusements and even assorted substances. Adherents, though, accept, enjoy, and put the interval between their wires to use.

Faults
We all have our faults and foibles. They're what make our human experience so much fun. The purpose of The Way is not to eliminate our faults but to make us aware of them so we can take action when they manifest themselves. This is where the patience to see our journey through to the very

end comes in. Time off our Path could see our faults overtaking us instead of us overtaking them.

Harmony

Some spend a lot of time disagreeing with nature. They fight nature and circumstance, and they fight others. Mostly, they fight themselves. These people are so far off their Paths it isn't even funny: they live fractured, scattered lives, never coming close to the lives they are meant to live. Their time on this planet is squandered. When their time comes to die, they will flail their arms and say "what if?"

You are living in harmony with yourself. Every aspect of your life agrees with the others. Your life is your truth.

Progress

Time spent lingering in one place or time – good or bad – prevents us from recognizing and accepting future challenges. When we turn our backs on the future, we are off our Paths and not maximizing our time or talents. It doesn't matter if we are basking in the glow of accomplishment or wallowing in something unconstructive. When we spend too much time mired in the past, our wheels have stopped turning. Progress has stopped, and we are marking time.

Time on your Path will make you adept at recognizing the beginning and ending of your cycles. You will exit each cycle gratefully: grateful for the good memories and attainments and, if the cycle was not particularly constructive, the lessons withdrawn. Either way, each cycle is used as a stepping stone to future accomplishment.

Subjective

Virtually everything is subjective. You accomplish or attain something long sought, there are, as the saying goes, a billion Chinese who don't care. Did you miss a mark you set for yourself? Perhaps someone is there to put it in perspective, that you failed at nothing and perhaps accomplished more than you had a right to expect.

One thing that is neither objective nor subjective is your Path. It is completely dispassionate because either you are on it or you are not: there is no middle ground and no gray area. You answer only to yourself because only you can put yourself on your Path, and only you can wander off it. Some may provide guidance, but we are the ones who must climb our own stone steps.

Movement

Adherents do not stagnate. They do not mark time or stand still. They move and they do because their Paths demand and see to this. They do things that benefit themselves and others, things that lay the foundation for future dividends. Those following The Way are always creating themselves.

Progress may be slow sometimes, but Paths only go forward and do not dwell on what has been or might have been. There are too many tomorrows to meet.

Conceal

Once you have some time on your Path, once following The Way is second nature, you will notice some changes: you've displayed the wisdom to identify your talents and what you are meant to do with them, the courage to utilize them and the patience to do it every day. As a result, you have become completely in tune with yourself and where you are going. Things that occupy others no longer interest you; things that used to interest you are now deemed superfluous.

It is best to keep these things to yourself. That's why personal experiences are kept out of this book: this is not a memoir; it is guidance for you to chart your journey. You must construct your own experiences, not live vicariously through someone else's.

Destiny
Destiny does not mean predetermination. We believe there are things for us to accomplish and that our Path will take us there. Our course, however, has not already been charted.

The only real choice in life is whether we are going to utilize our talents or squander them. This is why we remain on our Paths every day. Not some days and not others, not some years and not others, but every day because we know this is the Path to our destiny.

Freedom
Some spiritual disciplines require compliance, denial, and even deprivation. Instead of uplifting the spirit and the person, they crush the spirit and prevent us from utilizing every resource we have.

The Way, by its very nature, requires nothing except an adherent's goodwill. While compelling, it is not mandatory. Do it or not as you see fit; The Way will carry on regardless. The seasons will change, and your days will continue to pass whether or not you have found your Path.

To novitiates, the freedom of non-compliance can seem daunting. After some time on our Path, however, it becomes familiar, and soon enough you will find yourself demanding nothing less than the freedom your Path offers. Non-compliance with the dictates of external forces and declining to fit into the slots other people have assigned you are now second nature, resulting in the freedom to follow The Way without hindrance and with determination.

Rivers

Water metaphors have been a part of The Way since the start. Rivers follow a course not of their choosing and must follow the path laid out before them. They have no other options. In the fall, when there is little water, it does so humbly, going wherever its Path directs it. In the spring, when the winter snow is melting, water asserts its power and its Path can only provide guidance to its ultimate destination. Whatever the season, it accepts its Path willingly and naturally.

Similarly, we must accept the Path laid out before us. Sometimes, we do so humbly, and other times we assert ourselves. Like the river, our Path is laid out by nature, and we follow it to our ultimate destination. When the river reaches its ultimate destination, it barrels into the sea, having nourished everything on its Path. The same can be said of us; when we've reached our ultimate destination, we've nourished everything on our Path and made our time serve us.

Planning

Success in any endeavor consists of having a plan and executing that plan, and those who get on in this world have done just that. They have said, "This is where I am, and this is where I want to go," trusting The Way to take them there.

Of course, they had luck – both good and bad – along the way and guidance, too, but they have also accepted and embraced the responsibility and opportunity of constructing the life they were meant to live.

Manipulation

The Way may well be the only spiritual discipline that does not manipulate its adherents. Whether it's the threat of eternal damnation, the lessons of past plagues or floods, or a hero rising from the dead, there are always lessons designed to generate reverence and compliance.

In time, you may run into those who are interested in The Way. In this case, you must not offer external compulsion. Guidance is provided willingly, from the heart, and almost with disinterest because you cannot lift anyone else onto their Path. You have been allowed to walk the stone steps by yourself and you must insist on that privilege for others.

Ambition
Ambition can be consuming, which is why adherents tend to ignore it. Of course, we want to accomplish things, but The Way tends to remove a specific result as the ultimate goal. Everything we want is on our Path, so we must be careful to stay on it and let it show us what we are meant to accomplish. When this is done, ambition and the imposters known as success and failure are negated, and they do not hold sway in our lives.

Grounding
This is one of The Way's most subtle gifts. Almost imperceptibly, we go from seemingly being awash in a never-ending, always competing universe where we seem to be flailing and a half-step behind to an existence where, completely in tune with who we are and where we are going, we are calm and at peace. We live from the inside out, thoroughly grounded in The Way and ourselves.

Our only measure is the 24-hours we all have. We can use them on our Path or waste them. It's a choice we must make every day.

Acceptance
Accepting what comes is an interesting animal because, like some things in life, it is contradictory. For example, while

those on The Project tend not to fight matters, they do not blindly accept what others choose to spoon-feed them, either. They know acceptance merely means there are many aspects of life you cannot control. They know that if they have put an appropriate effort into something, the results may well be out of their hands.

However, adherents also know you don't strive merely for achievement. You strive to become your very best at whatever you are choosing to do. If achievement and notoriety follow, that is merely something else to be endured, secondary to the effort put in. The result is wonderful in and of itself.

Guarantees

There are no guarantees in life. The Project's great gift is giving us the focus to find what we are meant to do with our lives, but finding The Way is only half the battle. We must follow it. Even the the first tentative steps on a Path produce wonderful dividends of confidence and the expectation of a life well-lived if we are persistent and courageous.

Whether The Way was ingrained in you from birth or whether there were many years under your belt before you found your Path, you proceed knowing the only guarantee is a life of use to yourself and others.

Numbers

Despite our efforts to assign numbers to everything from air temperature to distance to velocity, the only way for us to project order on our lives is to reduce our lives to a single number: one. One is us. One is you and one is me. It's the number of lives we have, so it's the number of chances we have to live the life we want.

Now, as we've noted before, there are seven billion people in this world, and we can't establish order on all of them. In fact, we can't establish order on any of them except ourselves and we must take care to do that. We have one Path, the only number that matters.

Instinct

Like other animals, humans are guided in no small measure by instincts issued by Mother Nature, the biggest of which is the mandate to reproduce. It takes discipline to overcome this. No one is immune to this; we all have the same feelings and desires.

After time on your Path, however, you are completely in tune with what you will answer to. You are careful in answering Mother Nature's call to reproduce because you cannot maximize your time and talents if you are obliged to attend to an unplanned child or mate.

Adherents know a child is a treasure that depends on them not only for food and shelter but also for guidance and, most of all, love. This is why adherents are careful not to have children until it is clear this is part of their Path.

Difference

Adherents live different lives than others. Others sense this because even though they may not be sure why, they see the apparent ease with which you go about the work of passing your time. This does not make you better than anyone else, but it is a difference that sometimes repels others or causes conflict with those not on their Path.

That ease is the result of even a short time following The Way, work generally unseen by others, work that never ends but does become easier over the years. Those who ignore The Way, either consciously or unconsciously, have not put the same work into their life you have and will never achieve complete synthesis with their inner natures.

Totality

Totality is a word that pops up from time to time in studying The Way. Like other aspects of The Project, its meaning is both vague and precise. Vague because there is no objective definition. Precise because despite this, we know when we've achieved it.

Adherents seek totality. They want to withdraw every possible benefit from an experience, be it a brief or chance encounter or the sum of their time on this planet. They want to maximize both time and talent because to do otherwise means both are being squandered.

Totality means cutting to the very essence of our being and committing to finding totality with ourselves.

Road

We were all cut out to do certain things and those that get on in this life do those things. Those working The Project in particular recognize this and they have taken care to identify the talents they were born with and work to get the most out of them. We did this yesterday, are doing it today and will do it again tomorrow. We know no other way.

It doesn't matter what it is, either. All that matters is that it comes from the heart. Our only obligation while we are on this planet is to see our Path through to the very end. Once we have identified our talents and made the decision to get the most out of them, the life we want is there for the taking.

Due Course

We can't rush our lives. This is a lesson life is always trying to teach us regardless of whether you are on your Path or not: while we have no idea when our time on the planet will end, we must avoid human nature of wanting everything to happen *right now*.

Those on their Path, however, know they will ultimately be taken to where they are meant to go. If the journey is longer than we might have thought, it's because The Way has experiences it wants to share with us before we get there.

Confidence

Every success – even, especially, the small ones – prepares us for the next challenge, and before we know it, we're meeting challenges as a matter of course, attaining goals we've had both for a short time and a long while. The perseverance and diligence we've shown on our Paths have developed us mentally and physically and the confidence received from setting a goal and attaining it will provide continued inspiration in good times and needed guidance in difficult times.

Longings

When the time comes to evaluate our lives, we are not going to ask ourselves if we were sufficiently entertained, if we worked enough overtime, or how many members of the opposite sex we allowed to conquer us. No, at the appropriate time, we will sort through our lives and see how many times we were obliged to ask, "What if?"

Those who did well with their time on this planet will look back at few, if any, what-ifs. They chased their dreams.

Some they caught – life's great prize.
Some eluded them – life's great lesson.
Some they were chasing on their last day – life's great challenge.

Those with many "what ifs" will be looking back at time squandered, at serving masters other than their inner selves. They will be longing for what might have been.

Repetition

A drawback to any spiritual discipline is repetition, and your Path is no different. There are familiar themes throughout this book, necessary because we humans need reinforcement, especially when learning and trying something new.

Everything you read here comes down to one of three things. Those who get on in this life have the wisdom to know the life they are meant to live, have the courage to go and live that life, and possess the patience to live it every day. To merely have mentioned these once would not have done you any good; they must become second nature.

This repetitiveness is also one of the benefits. By reducing life to its most fundamental elements, you are allowed to cut through the cacophony of daily life and come face-to-face with yourself. While some stare into the abyss of what might have been, you stare into the depths of your soul.

Sailing

Those off their Paths can never quite fathom those on theirs. They cannot comprehend answering to your inner compulsion to act and to do. Though their hearts beckon them, they ignore this calling even as they mindlessly respond to whatever assorted outside influences tell them to do. Instead of putting to an open sea with a following wind, they choose to remain in port and watch others set sail.

Time

Time is an interesting animal. On the one hand, we all have 24 hours every day. What we get from our time on this planet depends on what we do with those 24 hours.

By this time you may find you are already dismissing time. You are realizing the only control you have is over yourself, and because you do not know when your time here will end, you do not worry about it; you are too focused on taking daily steps forward.

Patience

A person on their Path has done away with both time and fate. Adherents allow their lives to unfold without interference, relegating time and fate to stand off to the side and sigh, because they have no influence in their lives. What's meant to happen will happen when it is meant to happen. All we have to do is let it.

Exploration
There is no substitute for experience. People talk about doing this and doing that, but progress is not made until the first tentative steps in a direction or endeavor are taken. All you have is someone standing at the precipice, too timid to enter the void. Paths are not passive; they are active and should always be a place of exploration.

A common theme here is that our Paths do not guarantee the end of the rainbow. Those with the courage to explore their Path are not spared from tragedy or misfortune; they are only offered progress, the progress that comes from exploring and finding themselves.

Belief
It happens every day: people do this and do that in response to outside influences in an attempt to amuse themselves and put off finding and following their Paths. They are fleeing from what they are meant to be, life's great tragedy.

Those on The Project know their greatest thrills come from self-discovery and its attendant attainments. The more they believe in themselves, the more their Paths show them. Their lives have become their own entertainment.

Achievement
Some people think The Way is a sentence to privation and insufficiency. Nothing is further from the truth because

sometimes our Paths collide with accomplishment and, perhaps, notoriety. For adherents, this is treated in the same stead as everything else: it is put to work for them, just like every other circumstance nature presents them with. Benefits are withdrawn, and congratulations and perhaps adoration are endured. Achievement is merely your life's pass being stamped to allow you to proceed to the next cycle of your life.

Getting Up

The sport of American football teaches the wonderful lesson that when you get knocked down, you immediately get back up. It's a lesson useful to the new adherent, too, because it's not a question of if you'll get knocked down in this life but how often.

It's also a question of whether we stay down or get up. Whether literally or figuratively, we must get up every single time. Our Paths do not guarantee ease or luxury; they merely offer a way to climb the stone steps. We make this journey voluntarily, and it's not easy, but we must realize that every time we are knocked down, we have a priceless opportunity to get back up.

Perception

We've noted the auto-pilot that takes over those who are on their Path: they do what they are supposed to seemingly without thinking. As they should because they had the wisdom to know where their Path was and the courage to go and follow it.

All that is required now is the patience to follow it every day. You are no longer wondering what you should be doing with your life because you perceive it as a matter of course. You live your life as easily as a stream flows.

Sustenance

Other spiritual paths offer sustenance, too, but only The Project stems from deep inside us. Other paths rely on good works, some metaphysical assurances, or the prospects of paradise, with some waving the prospect of eternal damnation in front of their adherents to ensure compliance.

As we've learned, The Project ensures life is lived from the inside out. There is no grasping at spiritual straws offered by outside sources, and we never have to worry if we are measuring up to some deity's standard because the Ten Commandments are reduced to one: follow your Path.

Since you are now living from the inside out, answering only to your soul's dictates, your satisfactions flow from the inside, too. This gives you the satisfaction of knowing your Path is taking you exactly where you are meant to go.

Understanding
The Project's great prize is offering the prospect of, when our time comes to die, looking back at time well spent and a life well lived. We cannot depend on the prospect of eternal life in some unseen and unproven paradise; the only thing certain is our time on this planet. As long as we have the wisdom to know what we are about, the courage to live the life we were meant to live, and the patience to do it every day, we will have the courage to face death with the same courage and grace with which we faced life.

Aspect
There are two aspects to spiritual life. The first is inspirational, words that seem flowery, ornate, and sometimes archaic and are designed to appeal to our better and higher natures. You've read your share of these here, and we do not have an exclusive on this; they are common to all spiritual disciplines and religions. They are often the impetus to begin a spiritual journey in the first place.

The second aspect is the daily practice of a spiritual endeavor. This is difficult because providing the diligence required is exclusively up to us: flowery words won't help, and nobody can walk our Paths for us. We alone make the choice, and we alone must make the journey.

Flexibility

Flexibility is both a secret and a demand of The Project. Each day, we must be flexible and ready for whatever nature and circumstances put in front of us. This is not easy, and one of the things novitiates find supremely challenging in the early stages of their journey is letting go of trying to make life conform to what they want. They might see some short-term satisfactions, but forcing matters seldom yield any long-term benefits. Usually, all it produces is resentment from others and, ultimately, discontent for them.

Now, if adaptability is one of the demands, it is also one of the great prizes because being flexible does not mean surrender; it means triumph. Adherents realize that outside of utter disaster, there are very few circumstances that cannot be used to their advantage, and they use this knowledge to let The Way guide them better than they can guide themselves.

Magic

Adherents do not know magic; however, they do know themselves, both the ultimate wisdom and the ultimate magic. As you gain knowledge of yourself, you will notice the magic of circumstances that used to be annoyances are now being met with tranquility. Situations that used to cause fear are now handled as a matter of course, if they even pester you at all.

Patience

This is because those completely in step with themselves radiate peace. They march to a pace that may be as quick as others but is certainly less frenetic: while they might act with alacrity, they do not rush. Every action is in concert with nature because adherents act in concert with their inner self.

Perseverance

If you've made it this far, you've finished this journey. You had the wisdom to explore spiritual self-cultivation, the courage to explore your inner self, and the patience to see The Project through to the very end. If you apply the same wisdom, courage, and patience to your own Path, you will, at the appropriate time and probably fairly soon, be looking back at time well spent.

This will always be available for reference, guidance, and inspiration, but the work, of course, must be done by you. It is not enough to read and acquire knowledge, we must *know*. We must know what we are about so that we might know the life we are meant to live, and when we know this, perhaps we will know the patience to do this every day.

Few understand the journey to the center of the soul. The road to our summit is not straight, nor is it level, but hopefully this book has given you the impetus to become the driving force to climb the stone steps in your life.

AFTERWORD

This book came about from commentary I provided to some friends to whom I introduced 365 *Tao* by Deng Ming-Dao, a book that has provided inspiration and guidance for over 20 years. My copy was given to me by an old buddy who was long ago lost touch with, is held together with a rubber band, and it is a pleasure to refer it to you.

I've lived every lesson offered in this book. My hope is you give yourself the opportunity to do this, too.

Cordially, and with every good wish,
Gaylon
Somewhere in the Rockies
Summer, 2024

www.ingramcontent.com/pod-product-compliance
Lightning Source LLC
Chambersburg PA
CBHW030232100526
44583CB00013BA/912